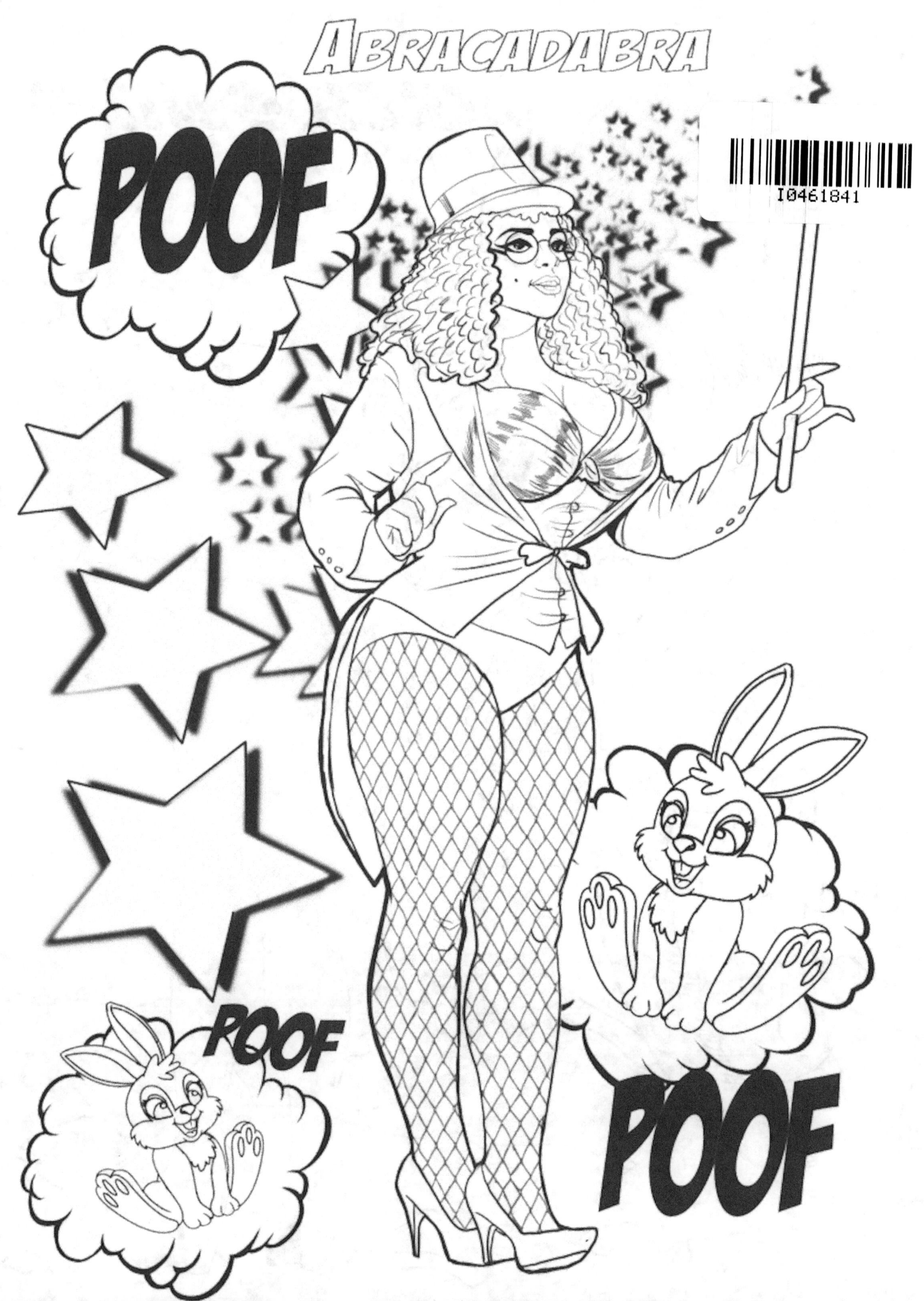

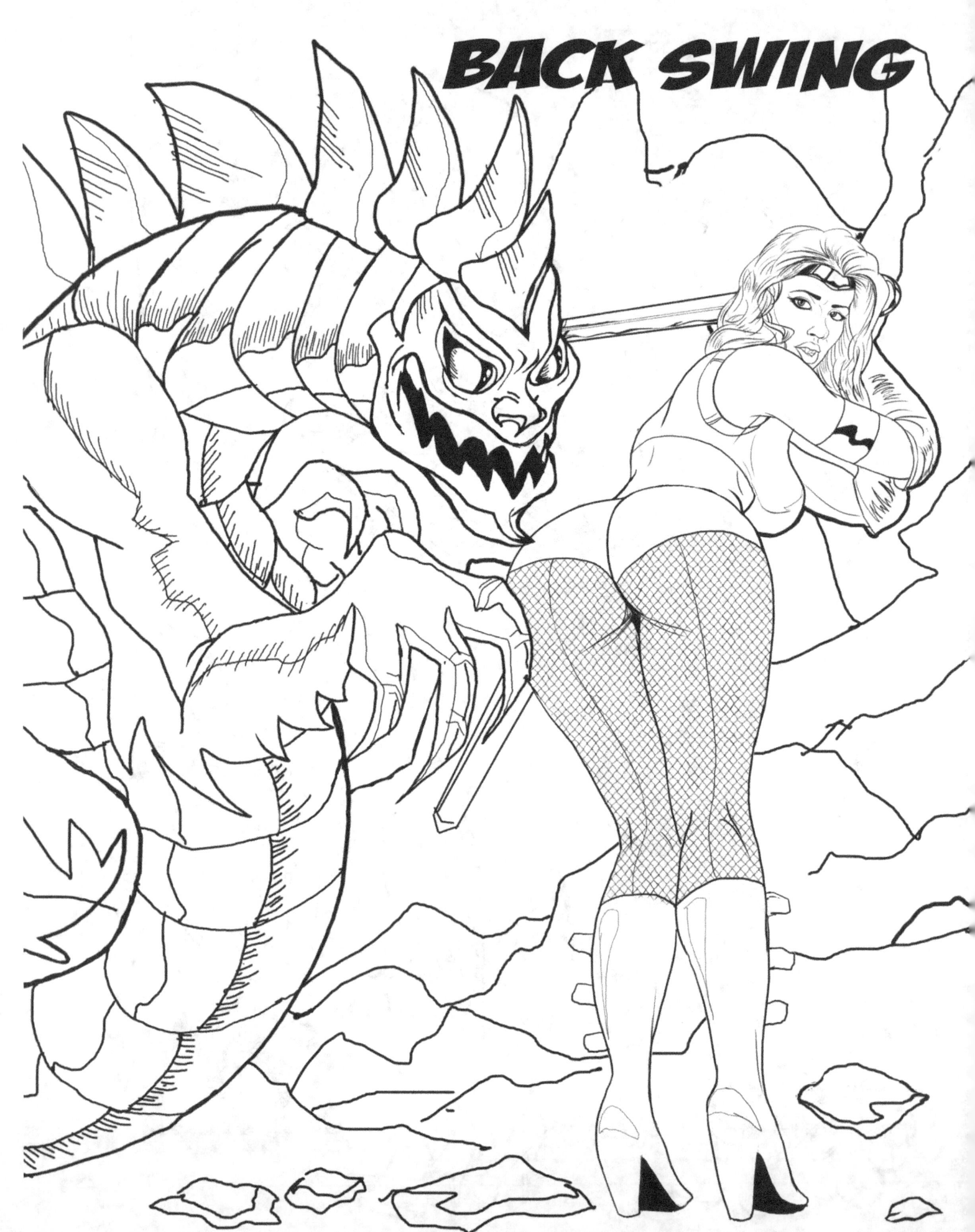

BACK SWING

# CURVATURE OF SPACE

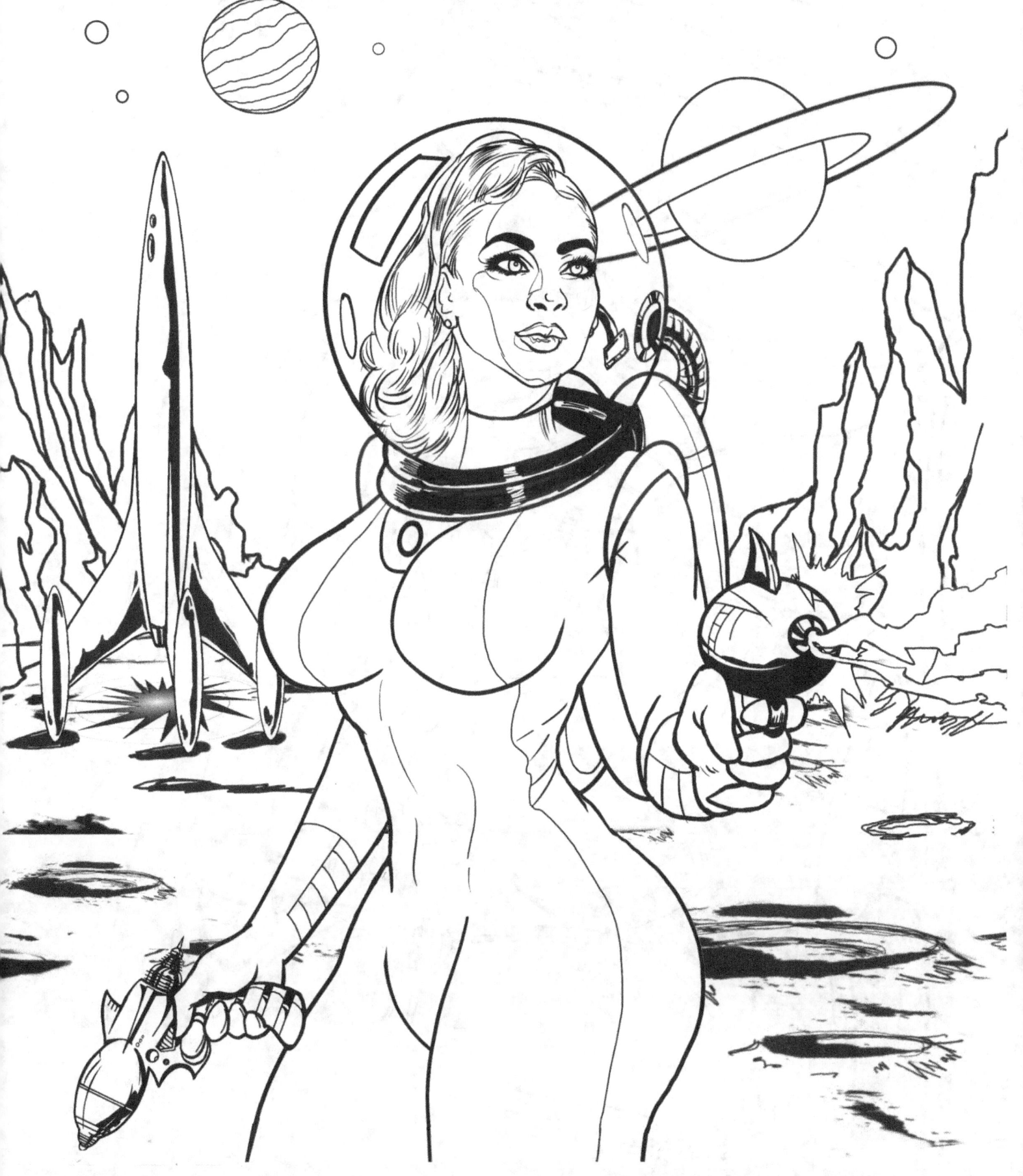

# DRACULA ENTERS

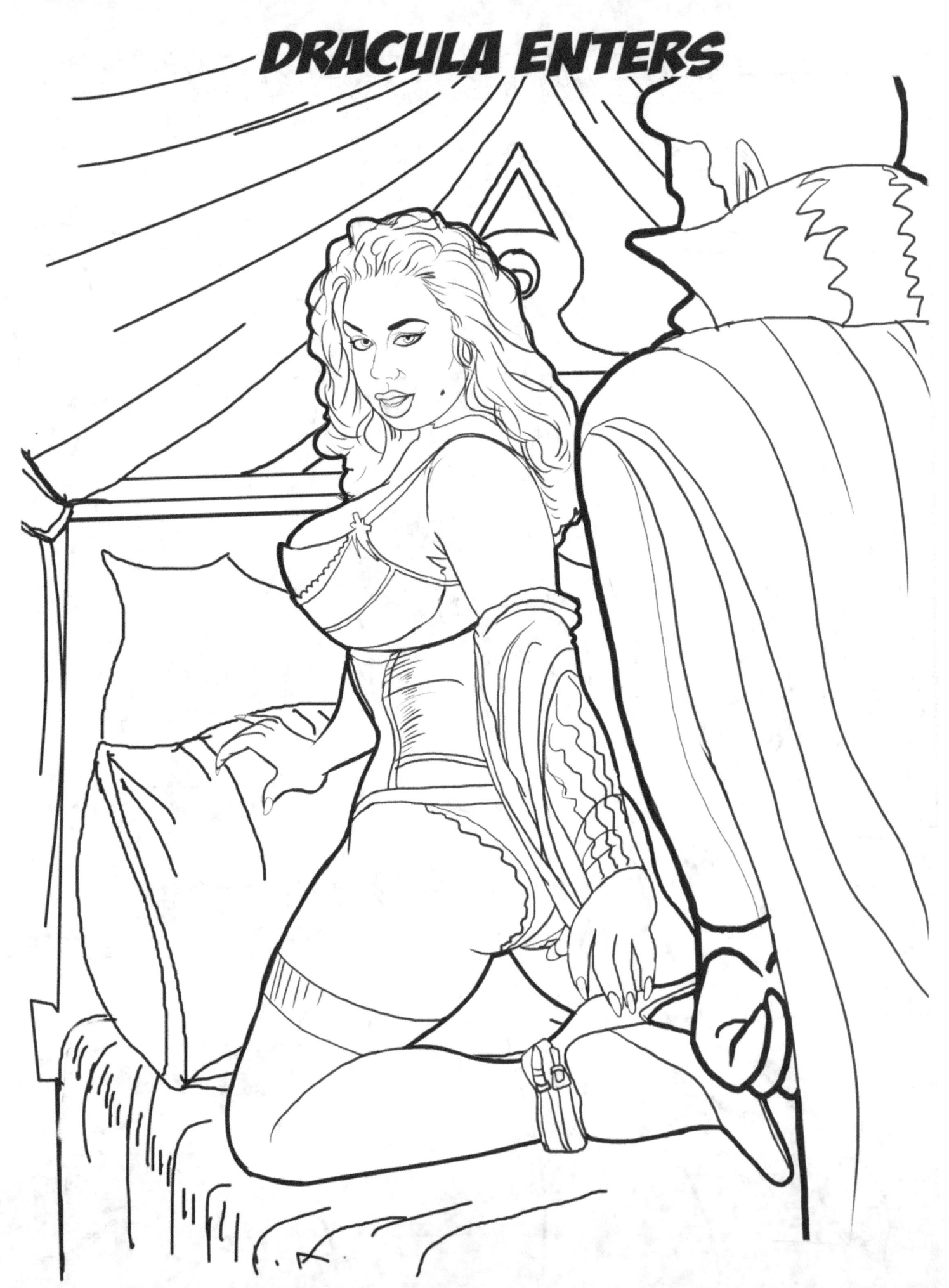

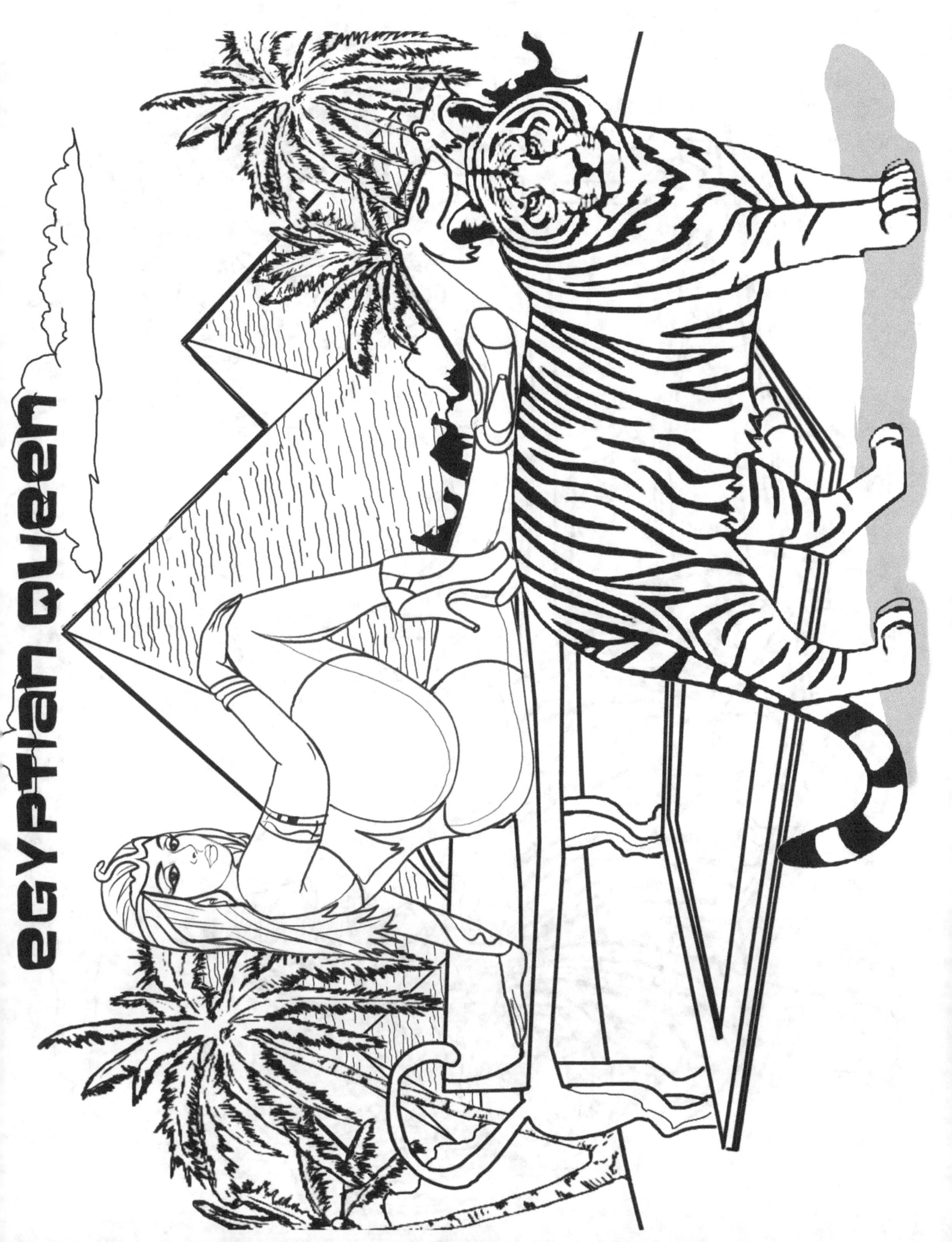

EGYPTIAN QUEEN

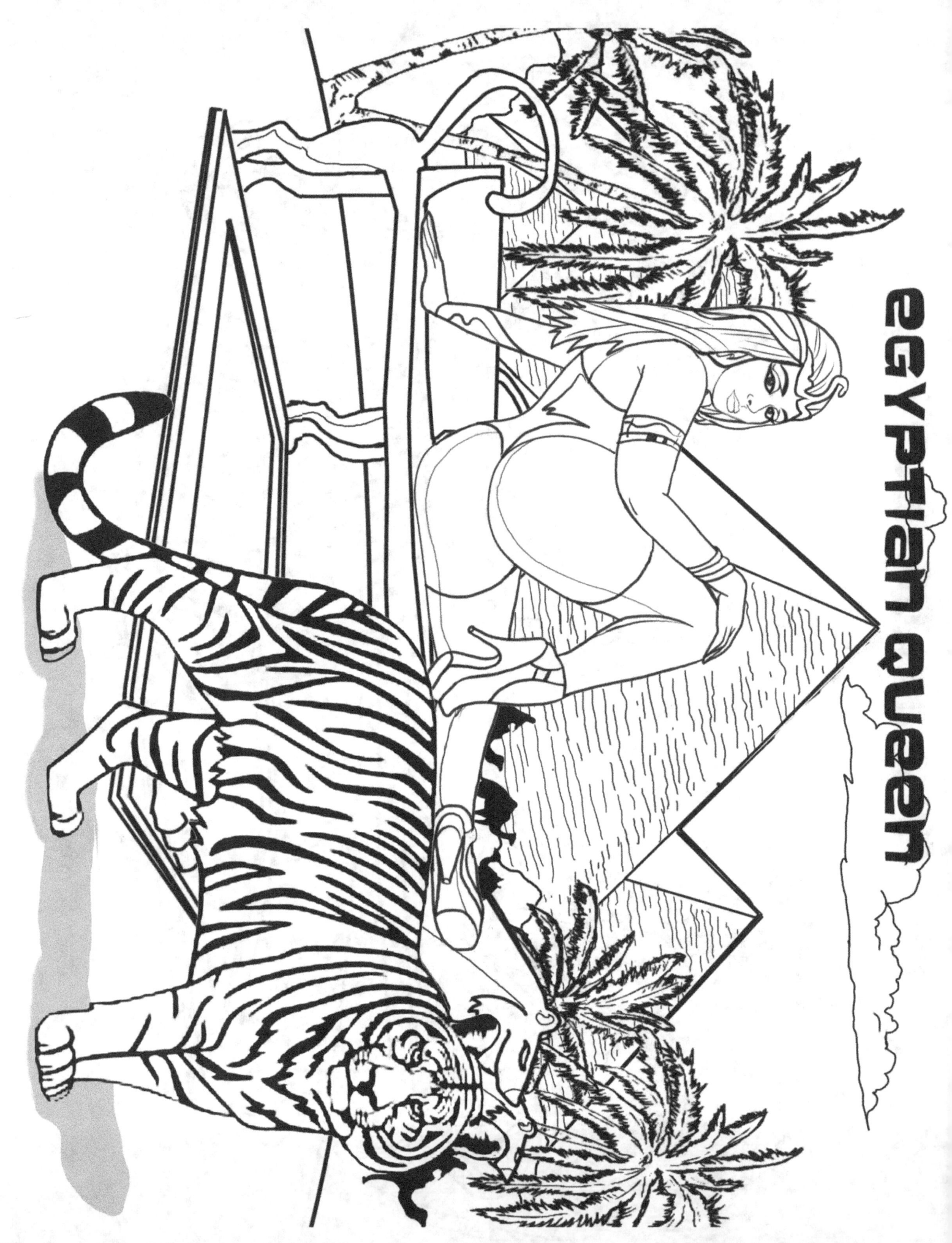

egyptian queen

# EVENING IN THE GARDEN

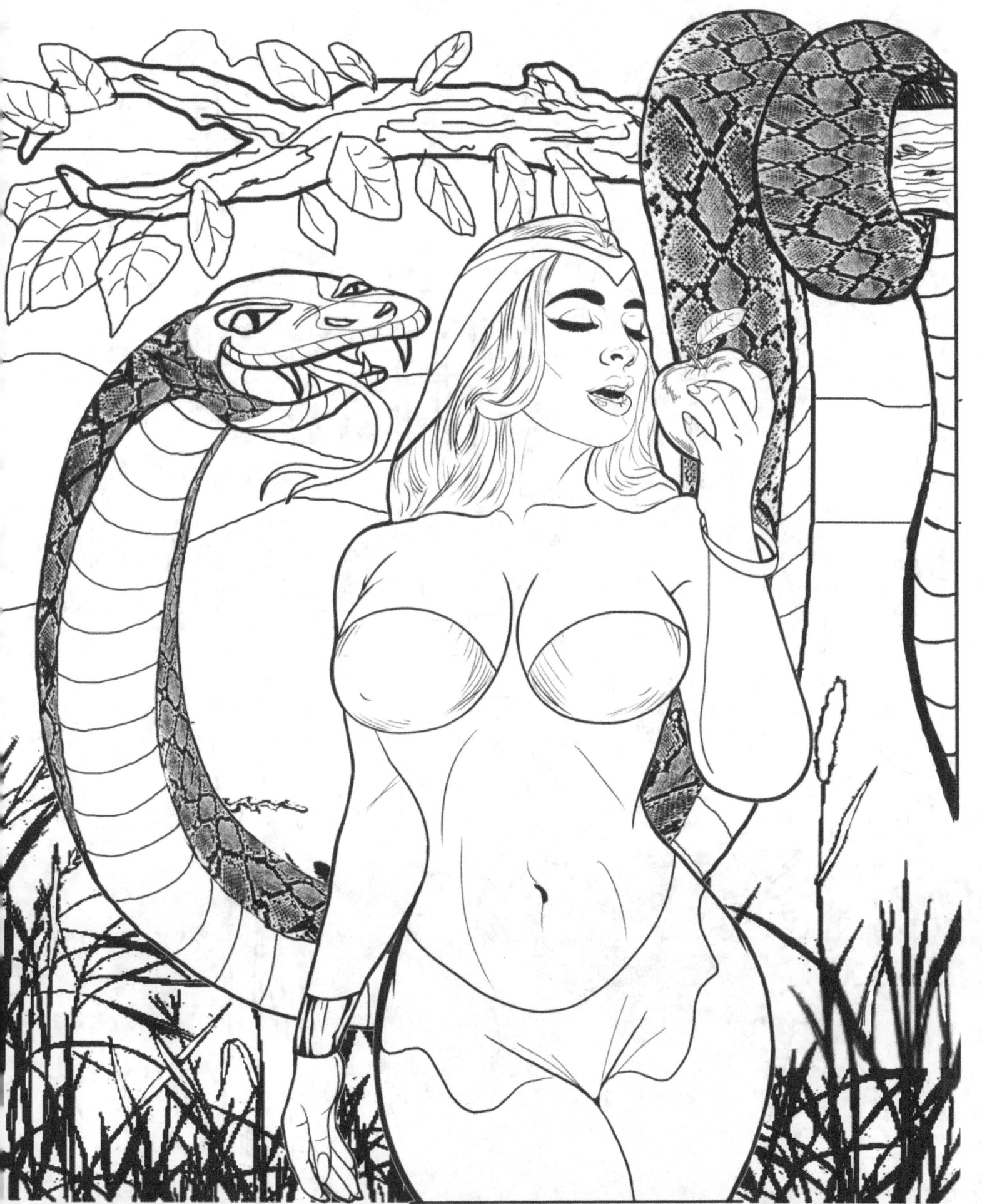

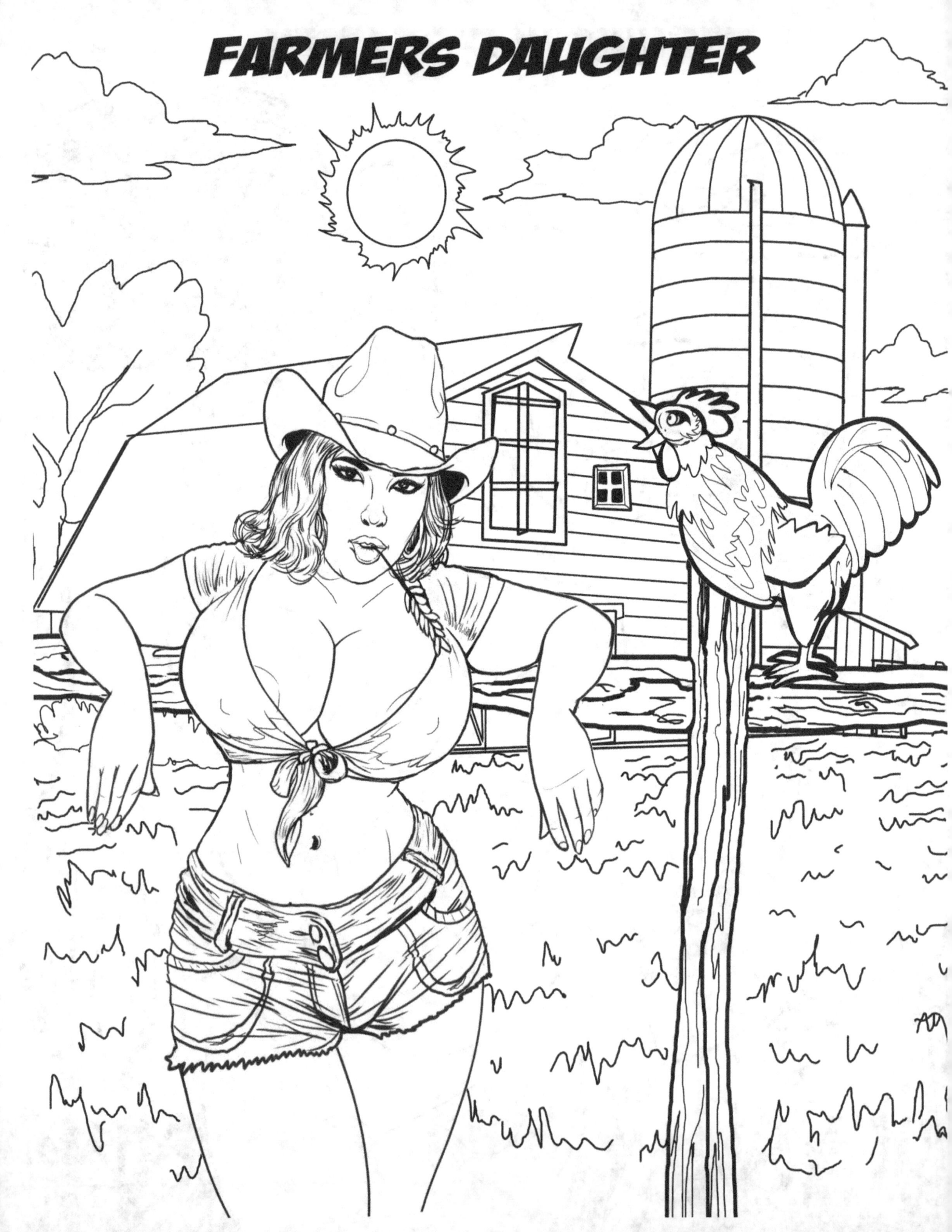

# FLAMIN' CROSSBOW

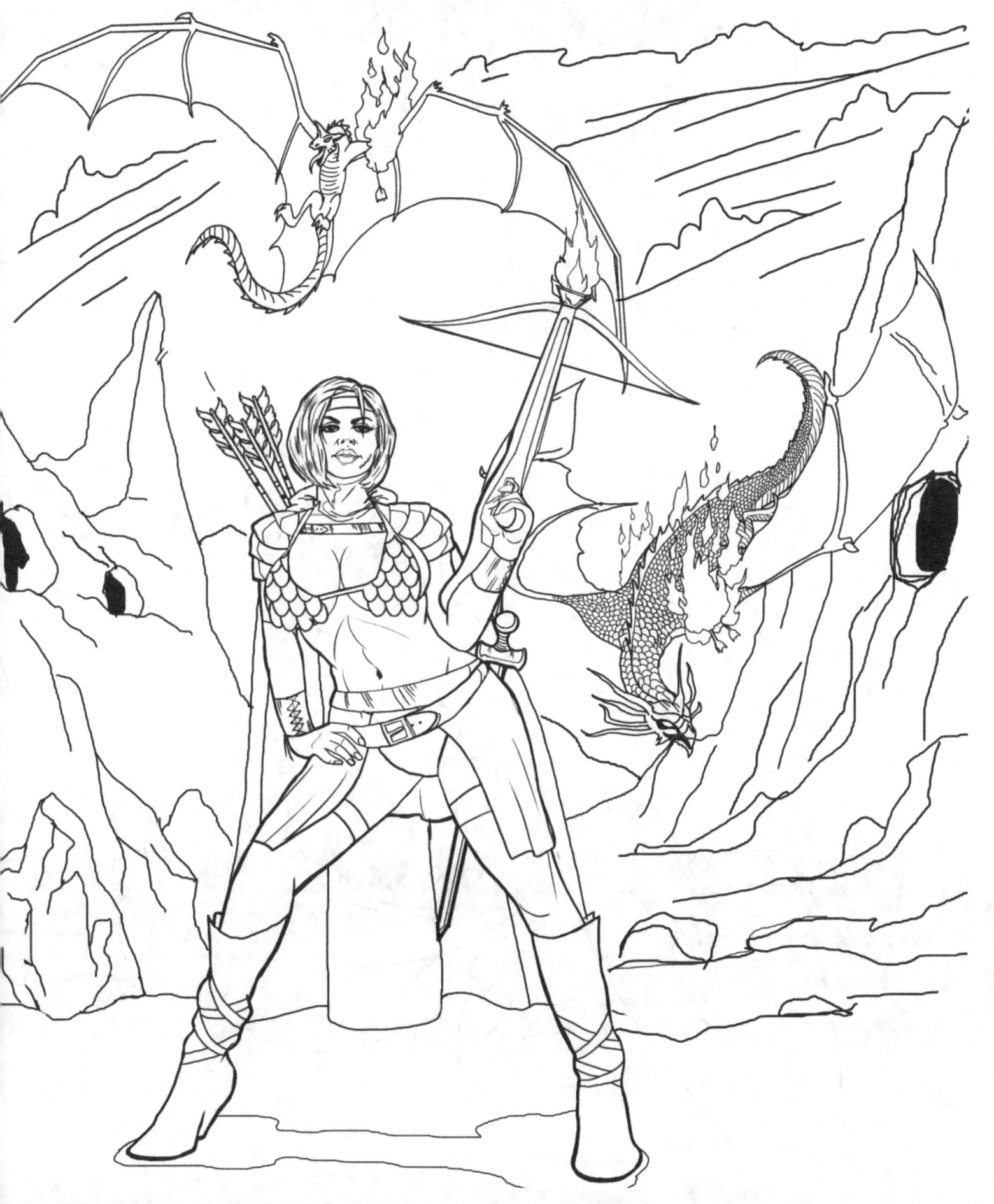

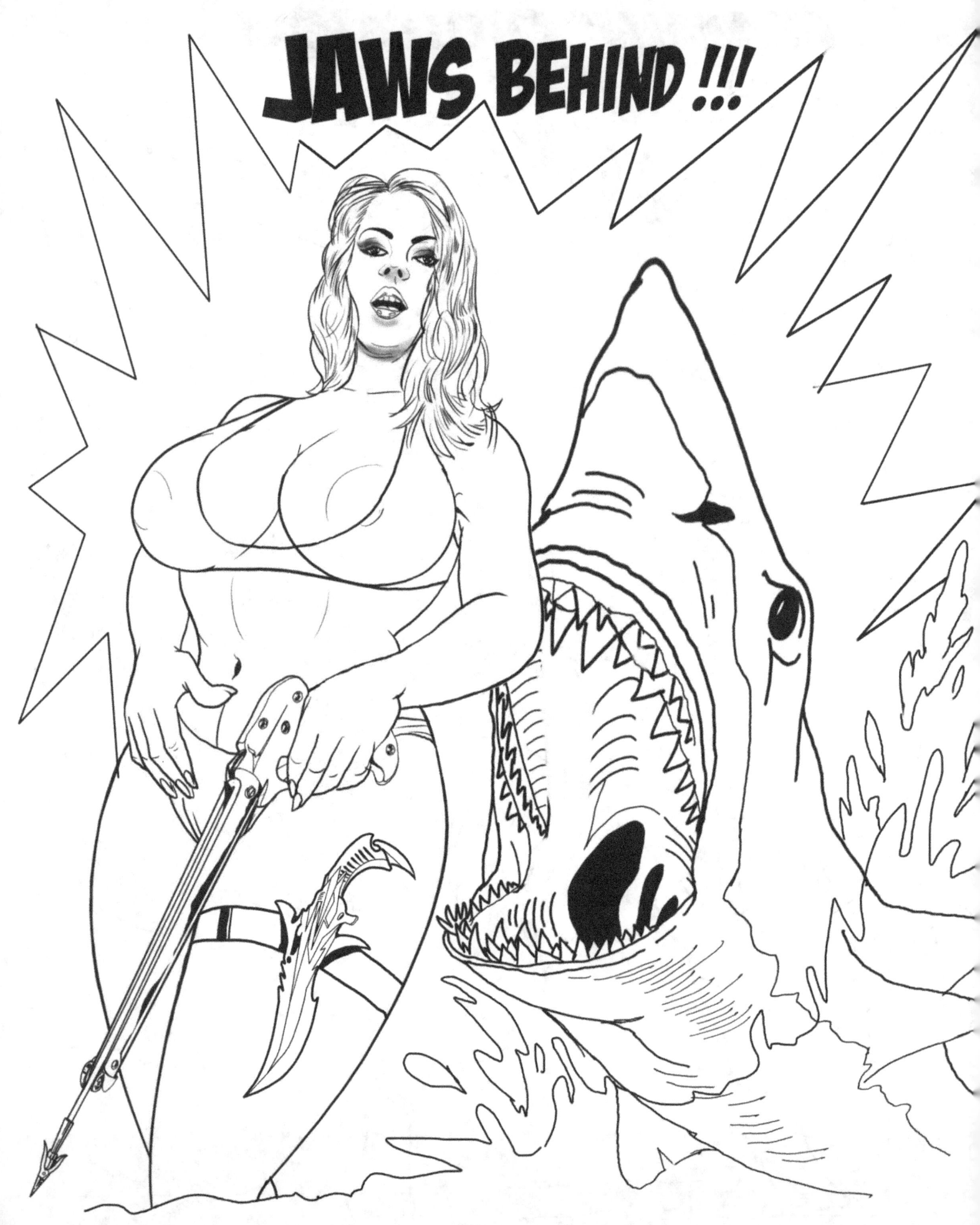

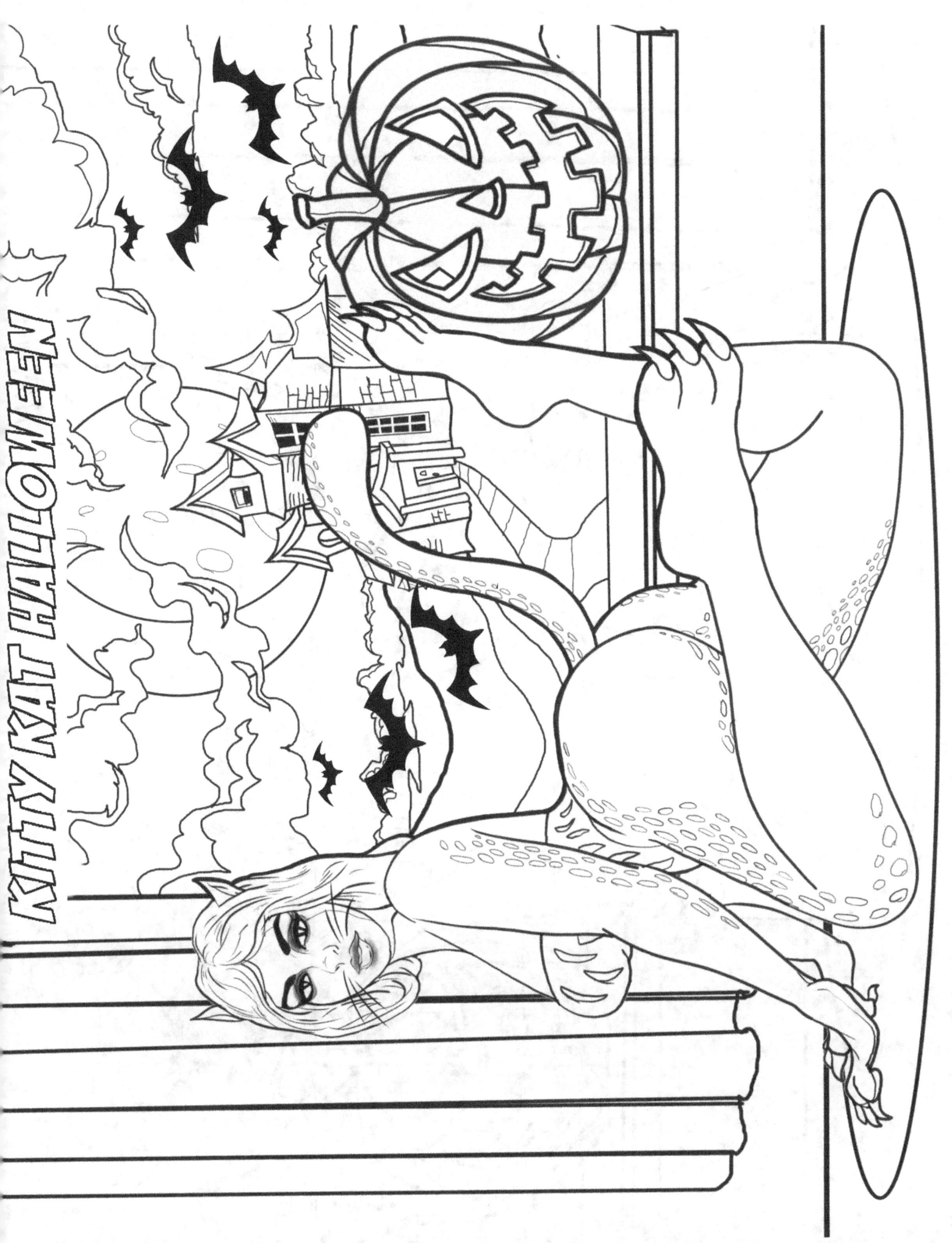

KITTY KAT HALLOWEEN

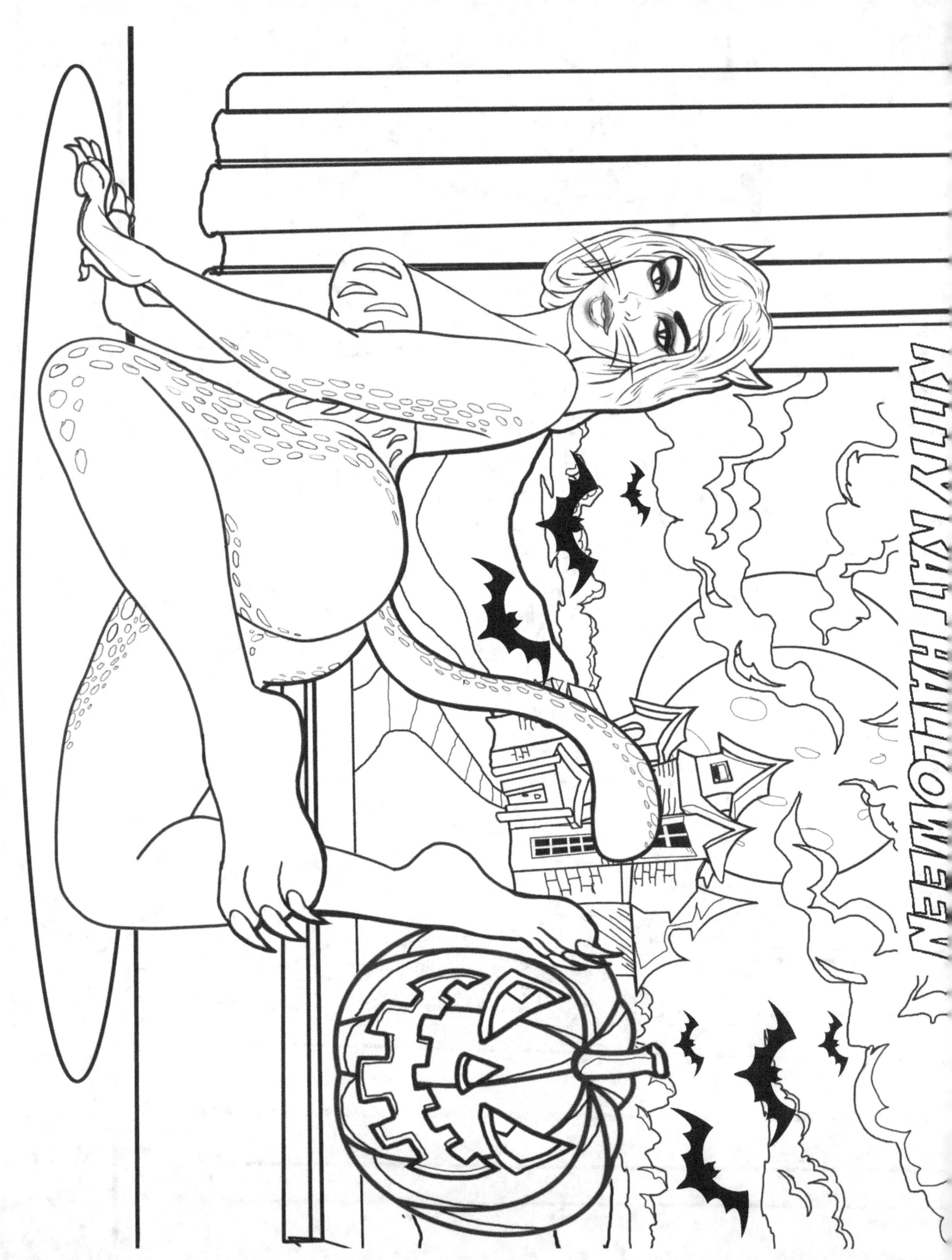

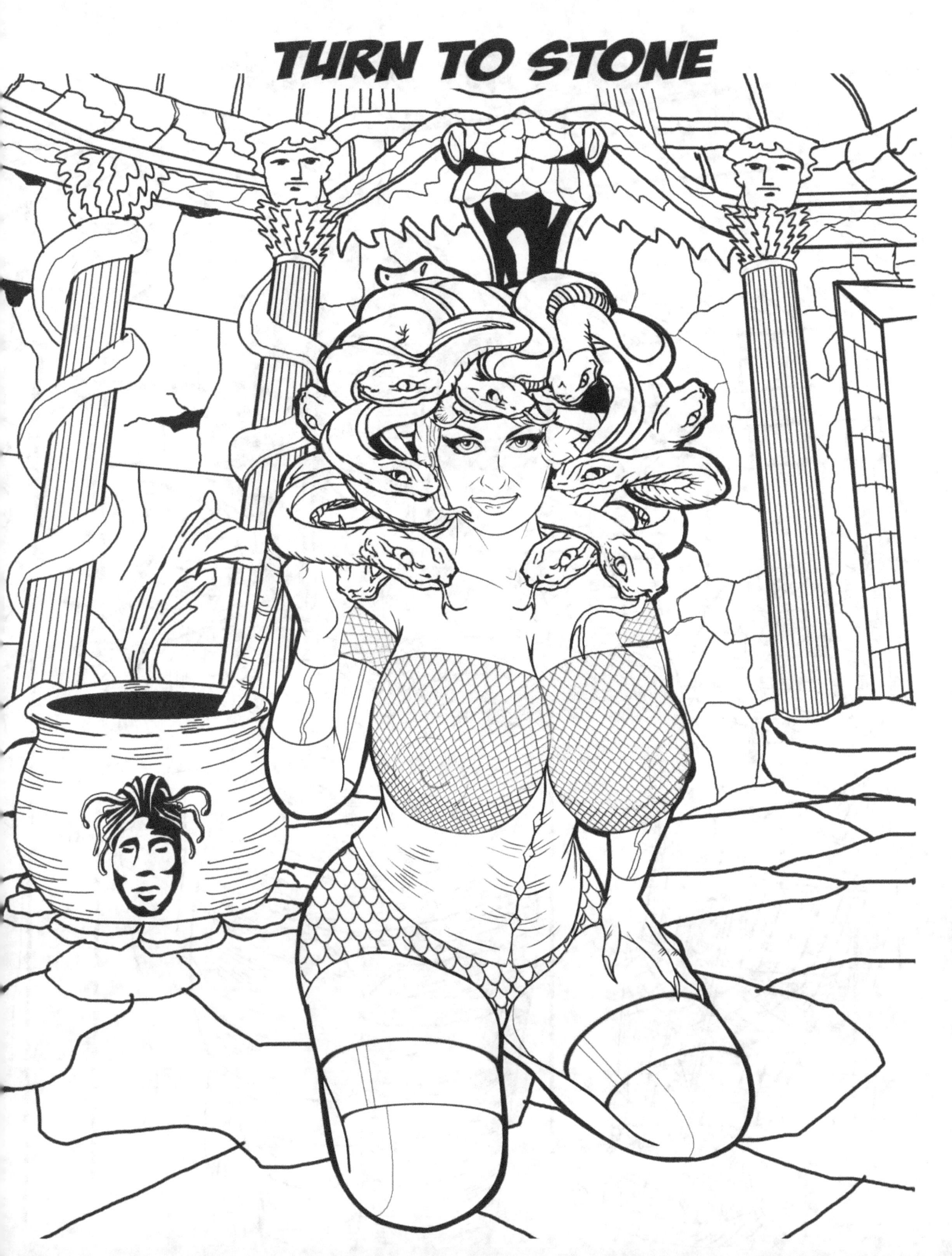

# TURN TO STONE

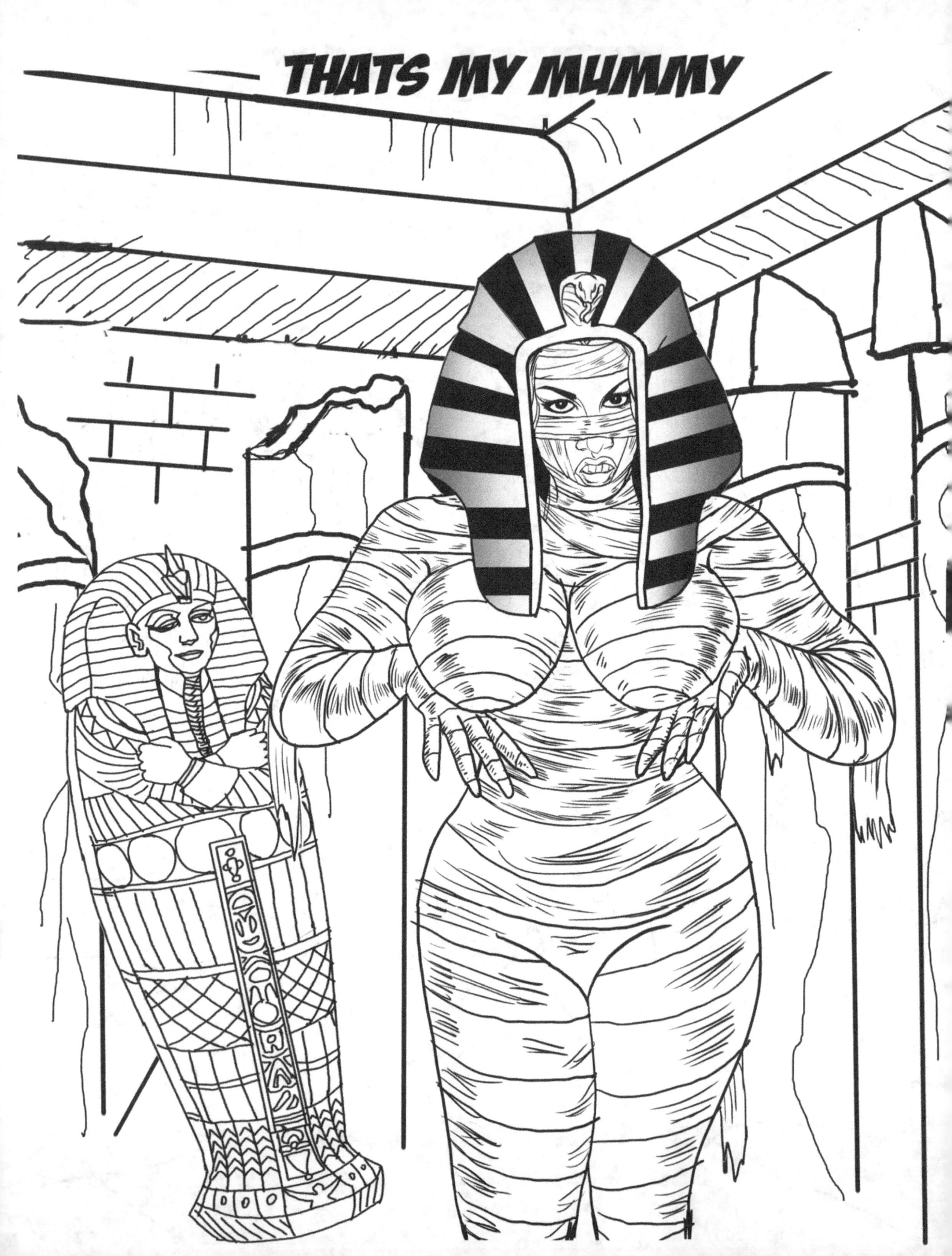

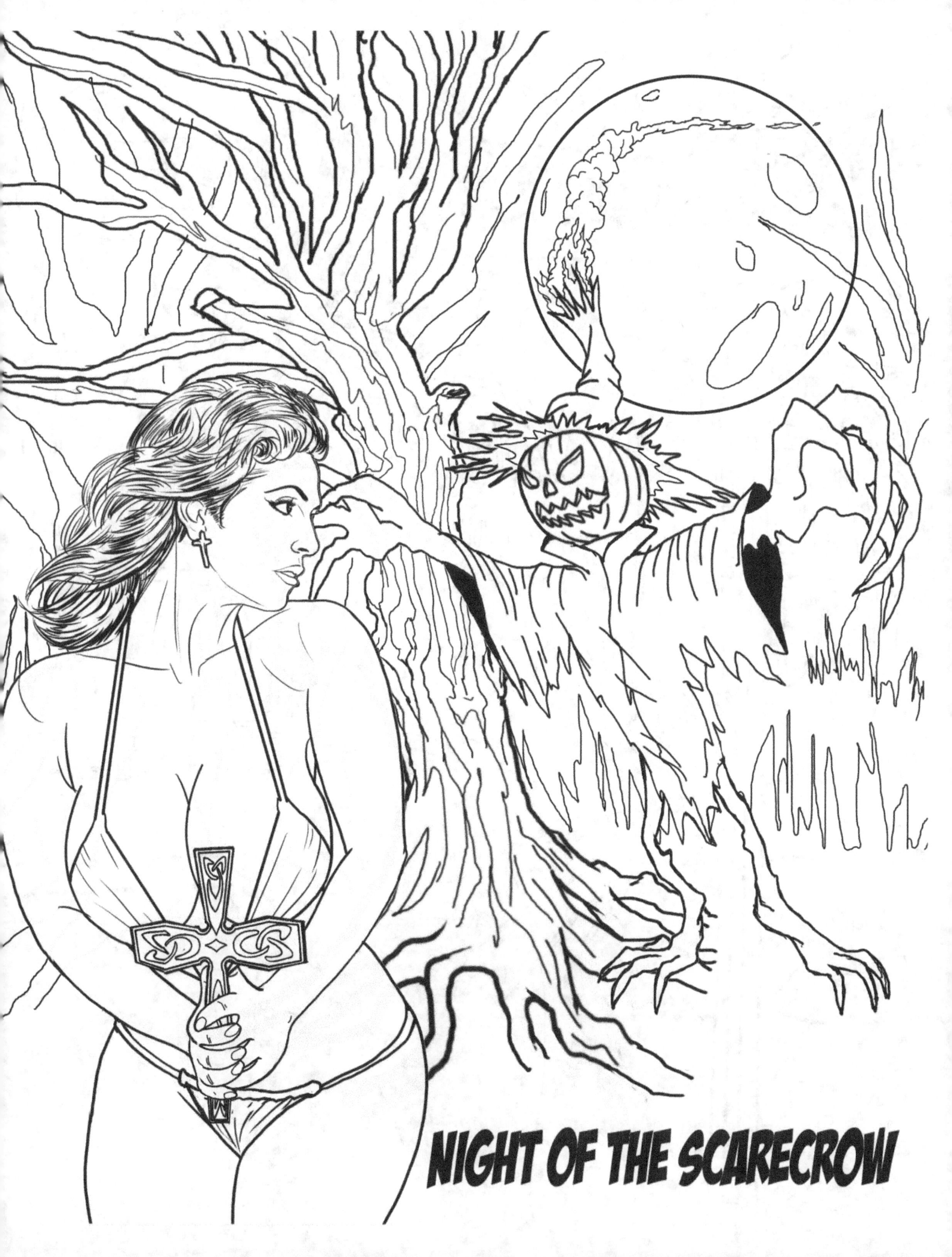

NIGHT OF THE SCARECROW

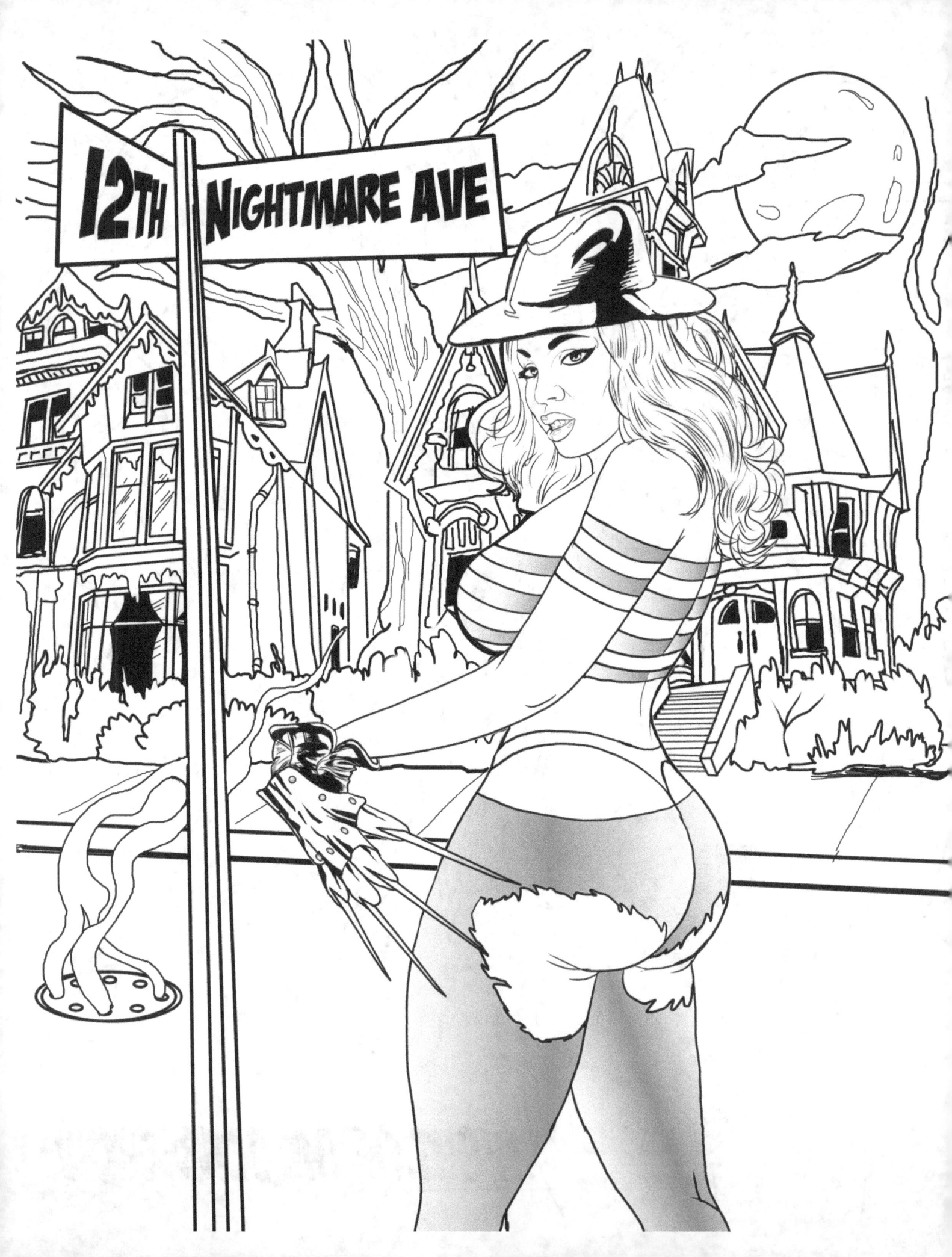

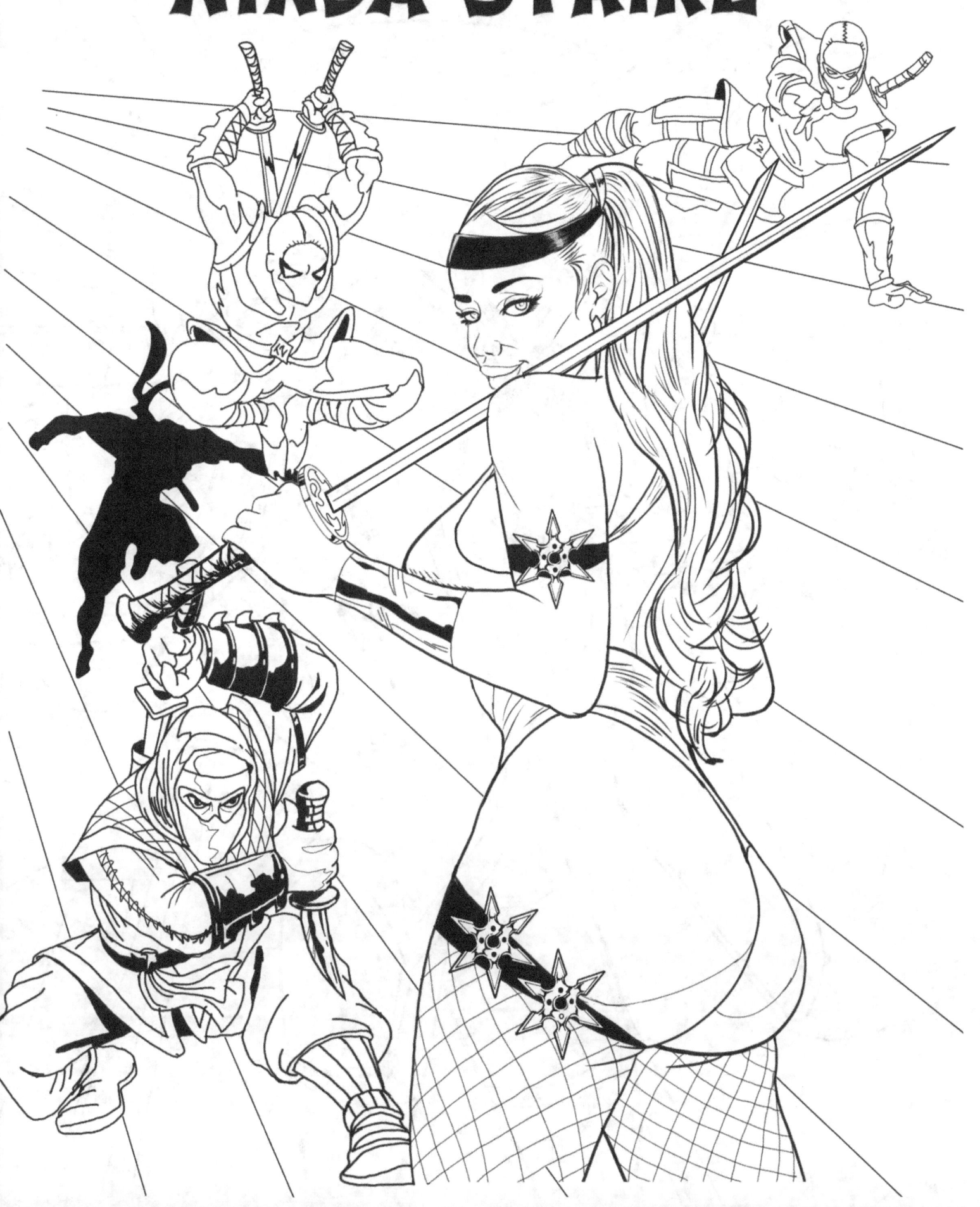

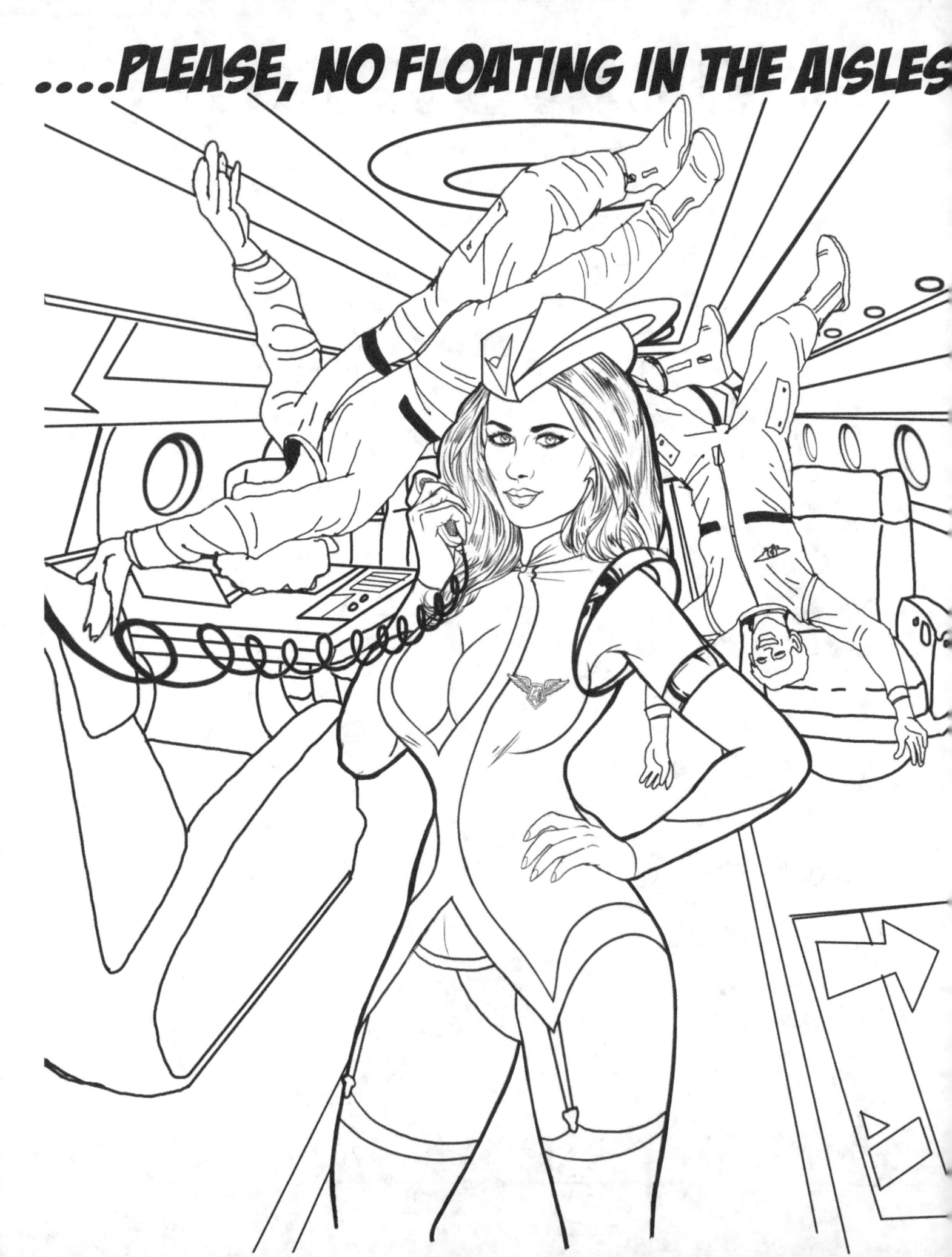

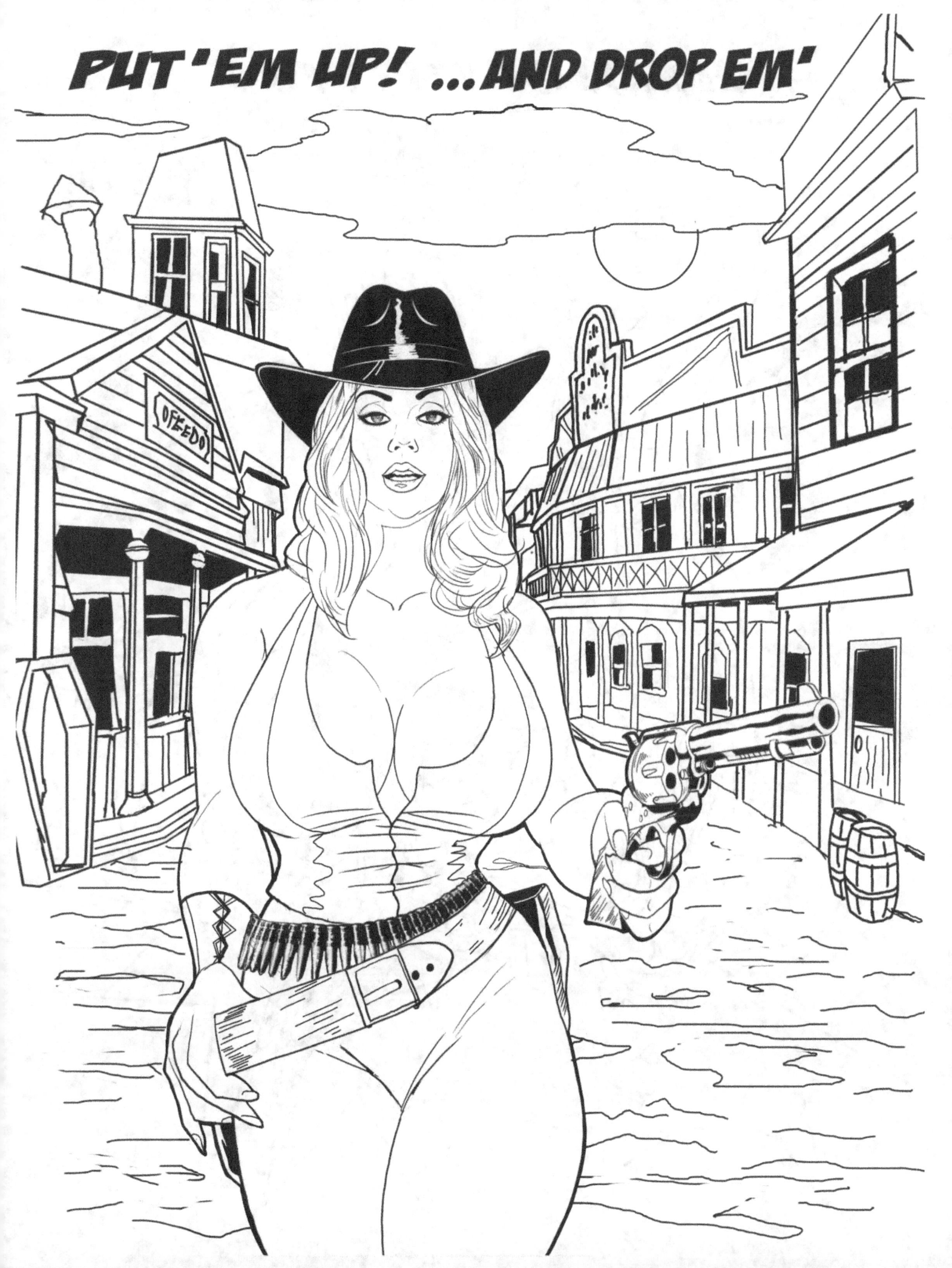

# QUEEN OF THE BATS

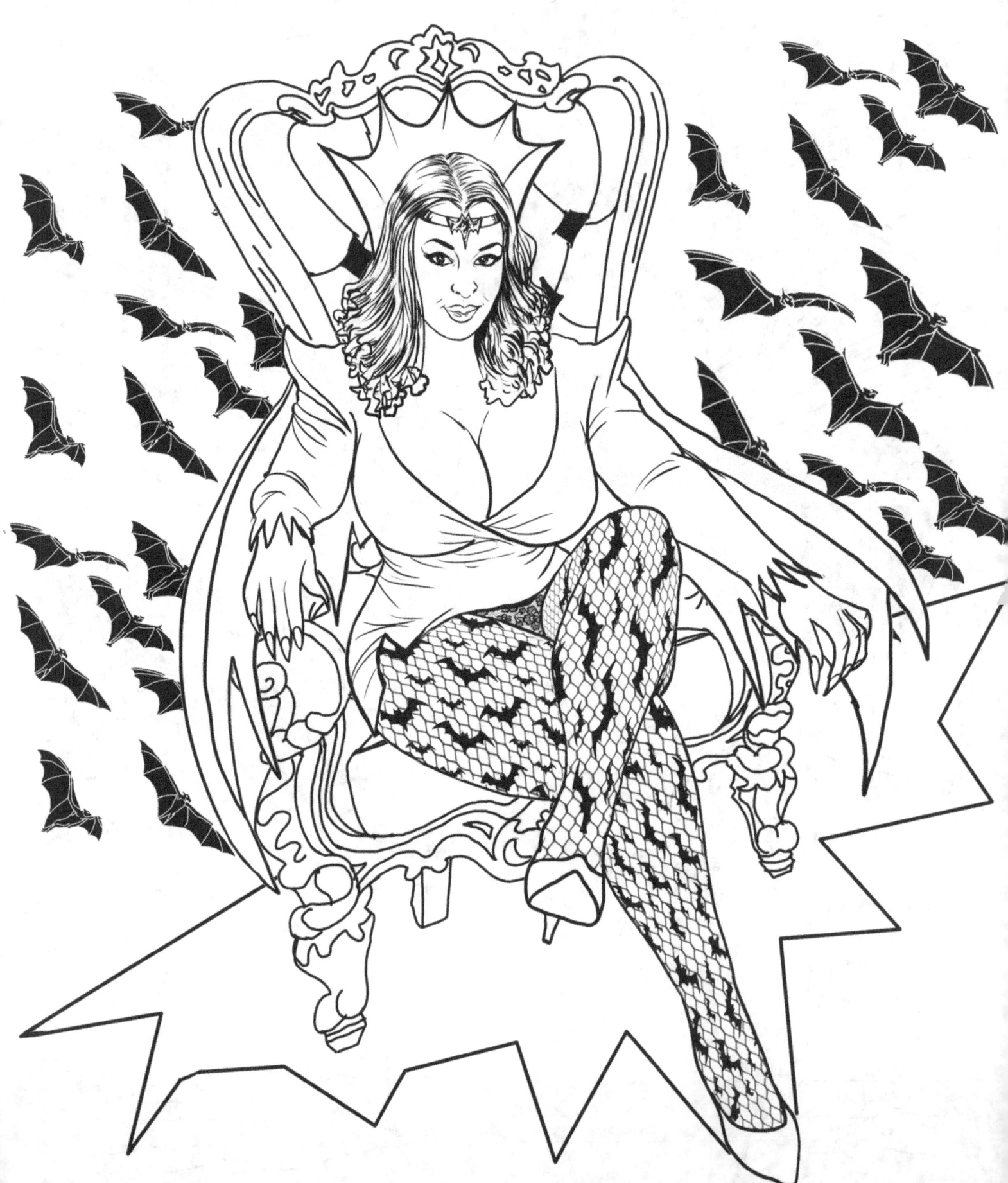

# READY FOR DUTY

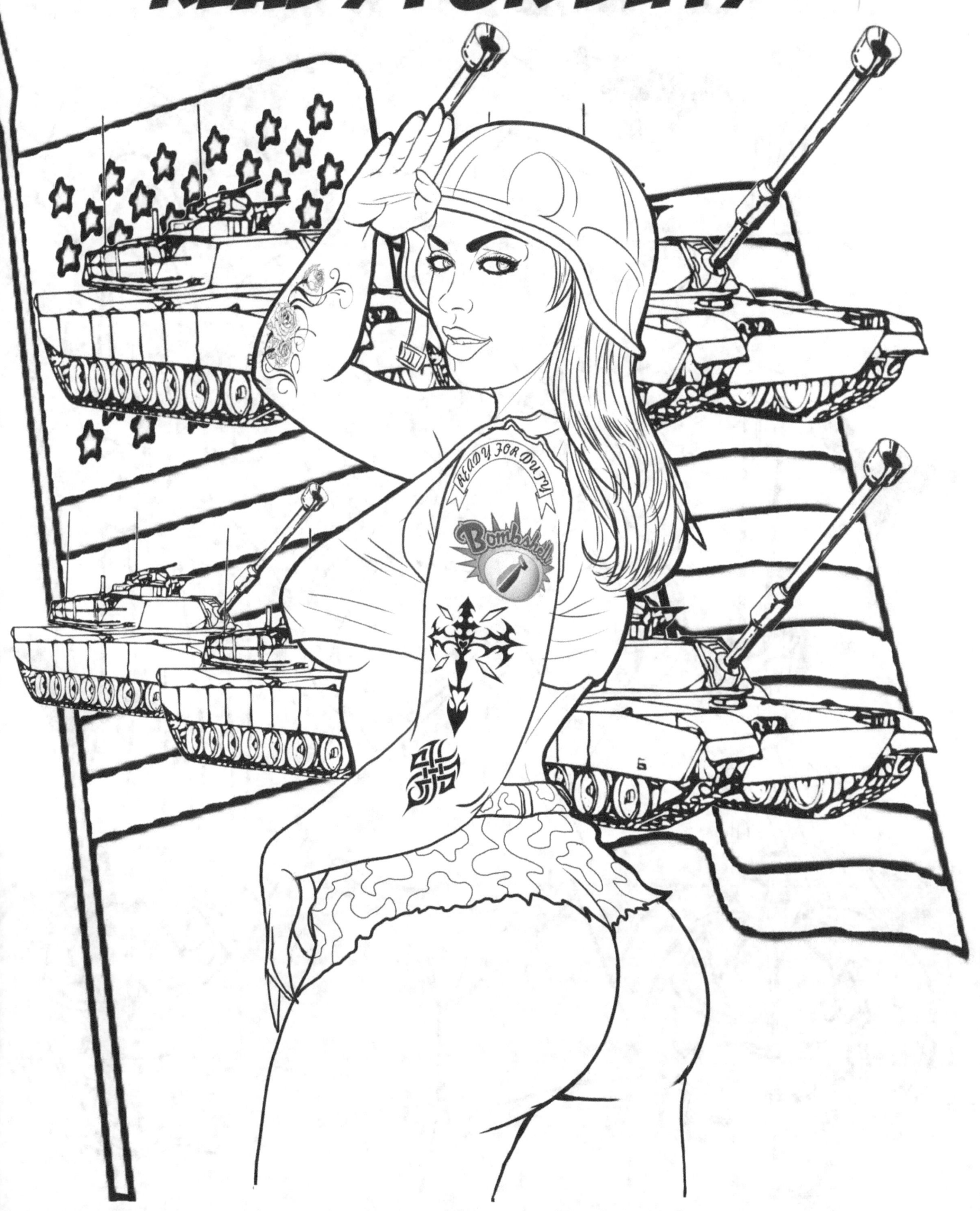

# I'M TOO READY FOR HALLOWEEN

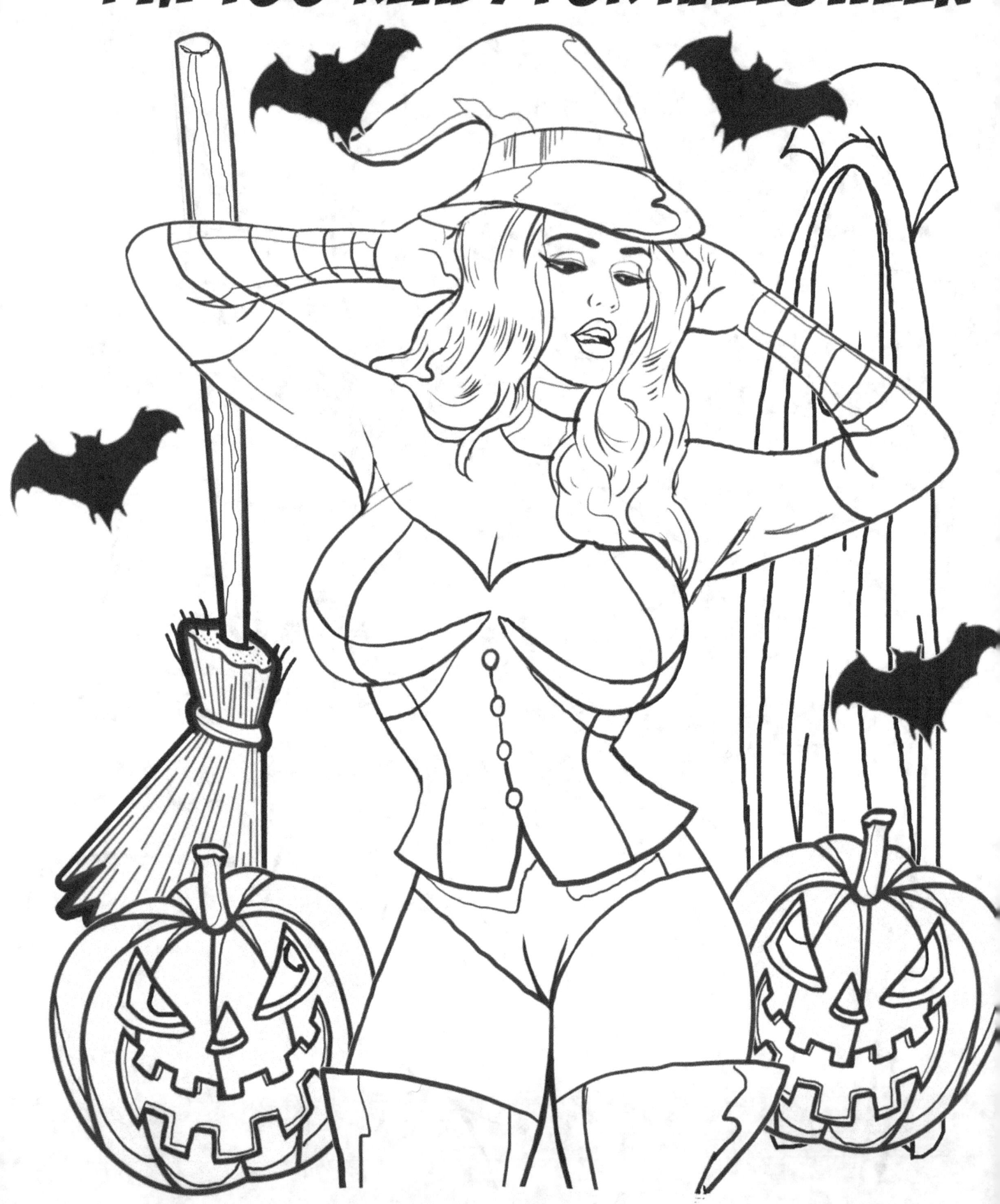

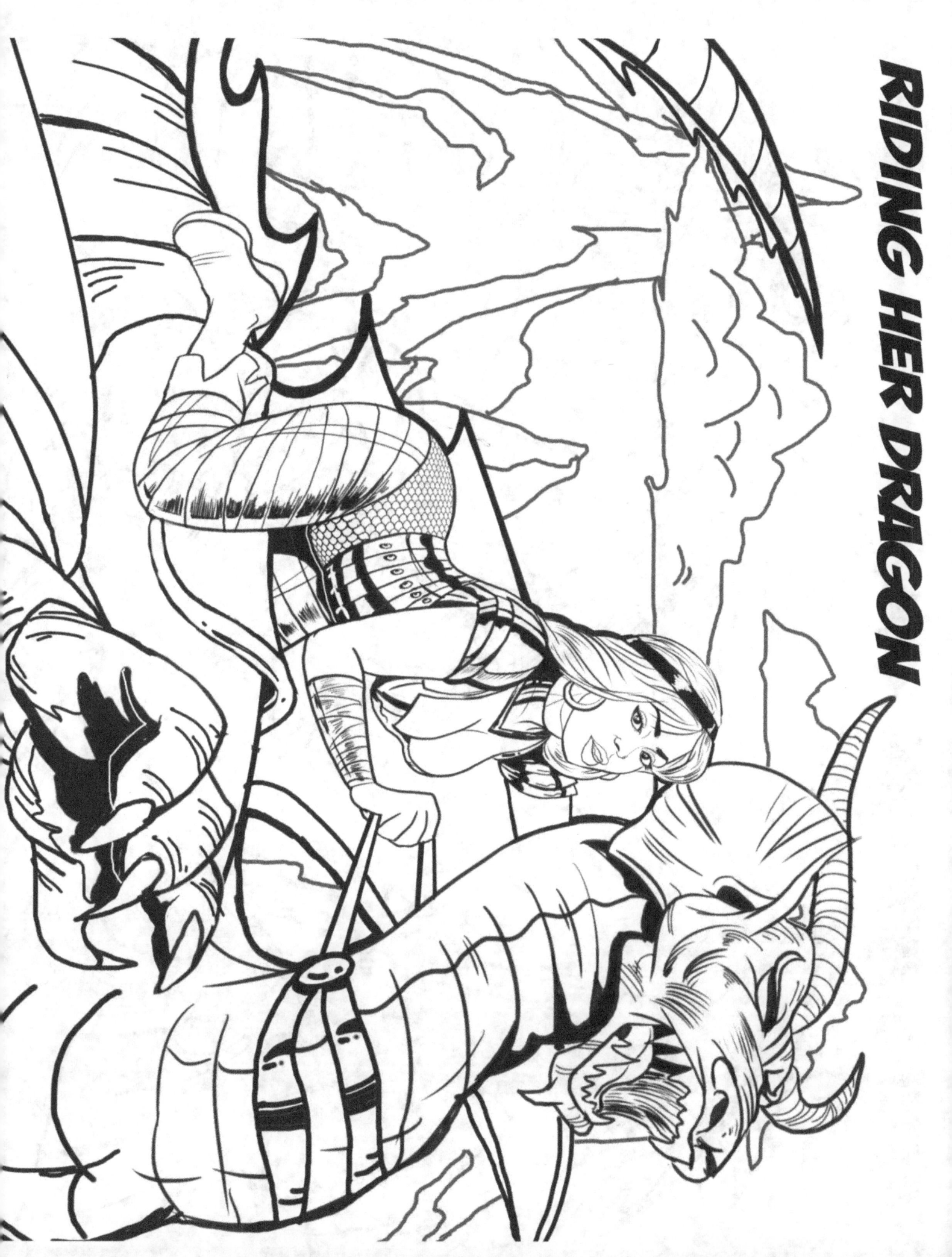

RIDING HER DRAGON

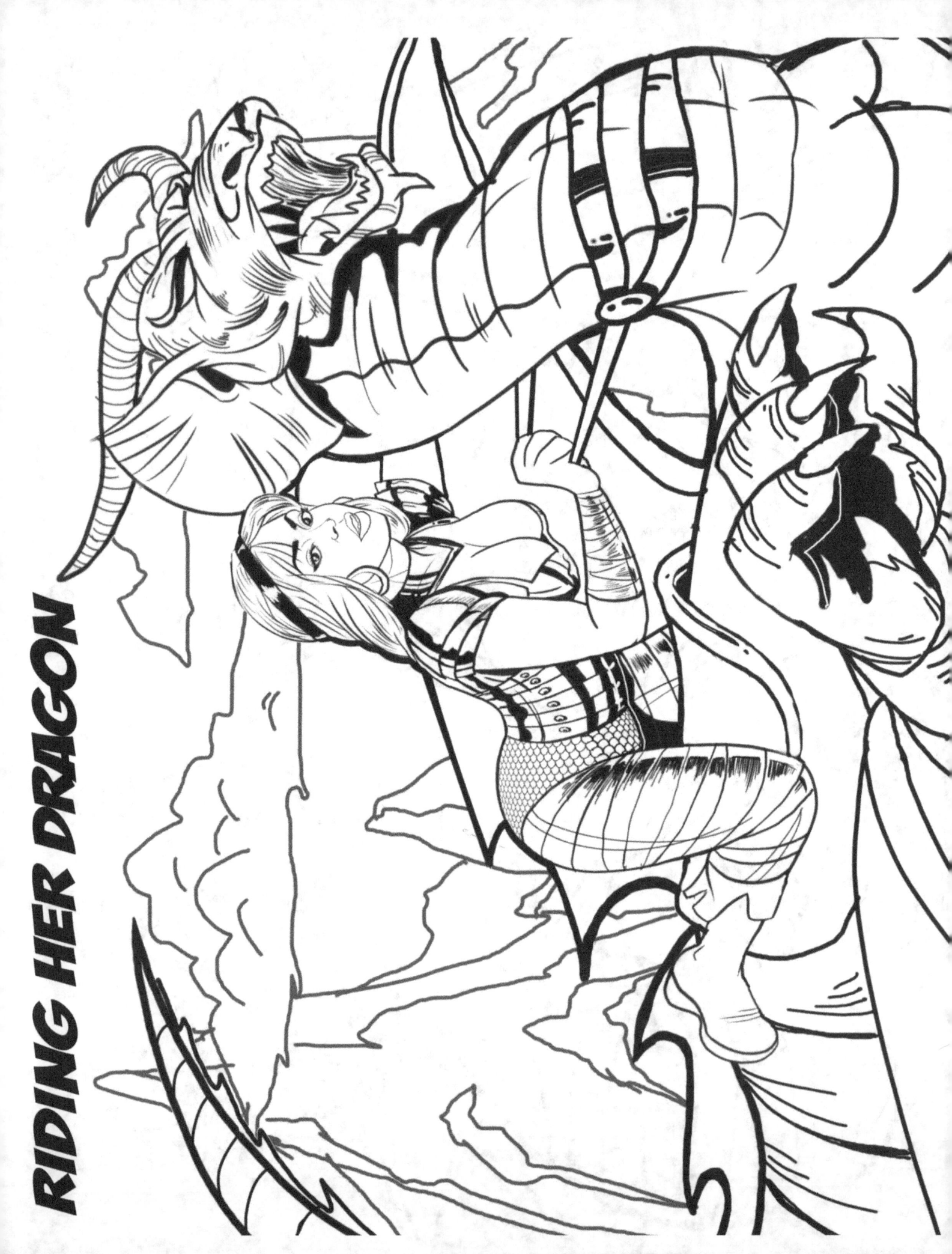

RIDING HER DRAGON

# DRAGON SWORD

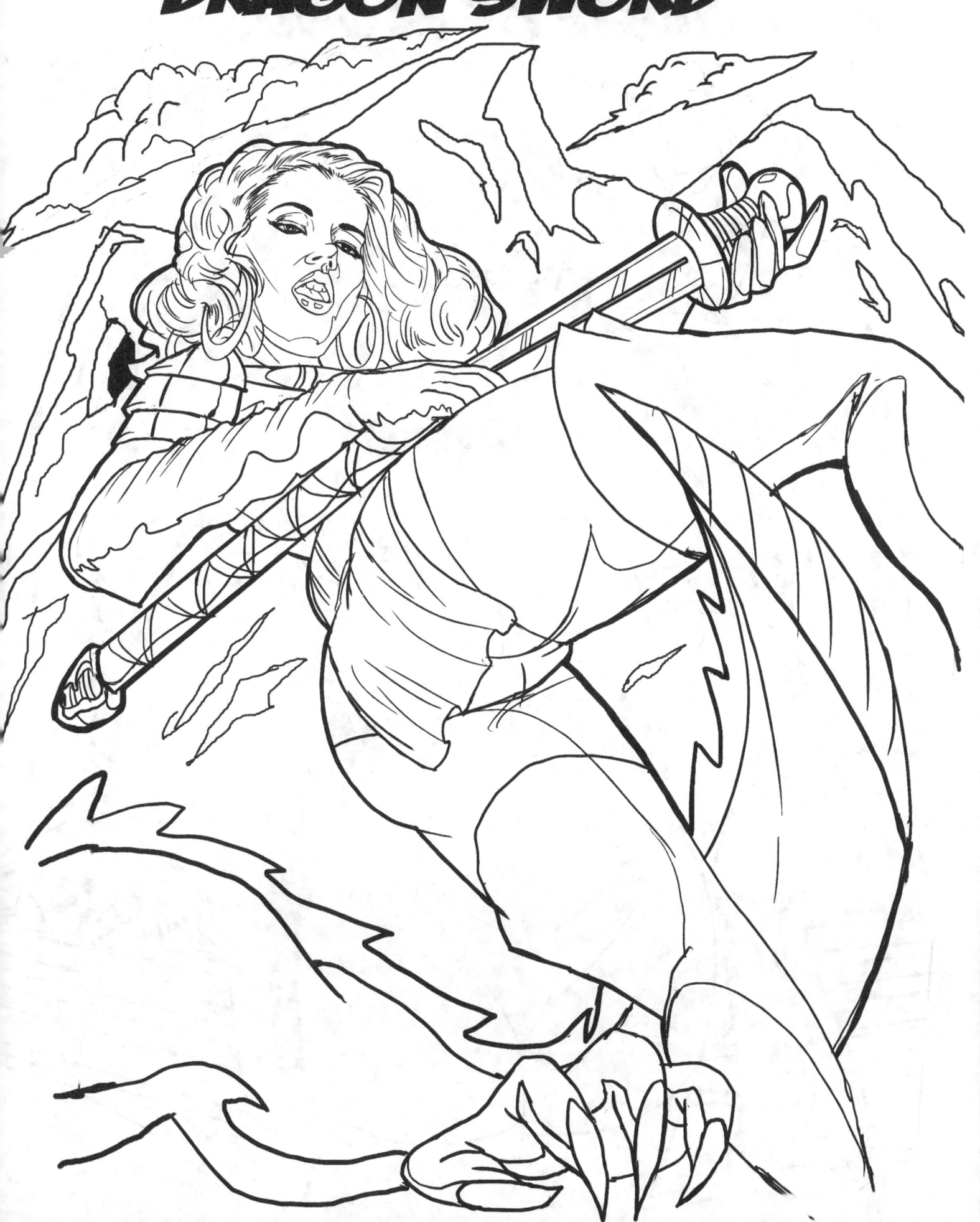

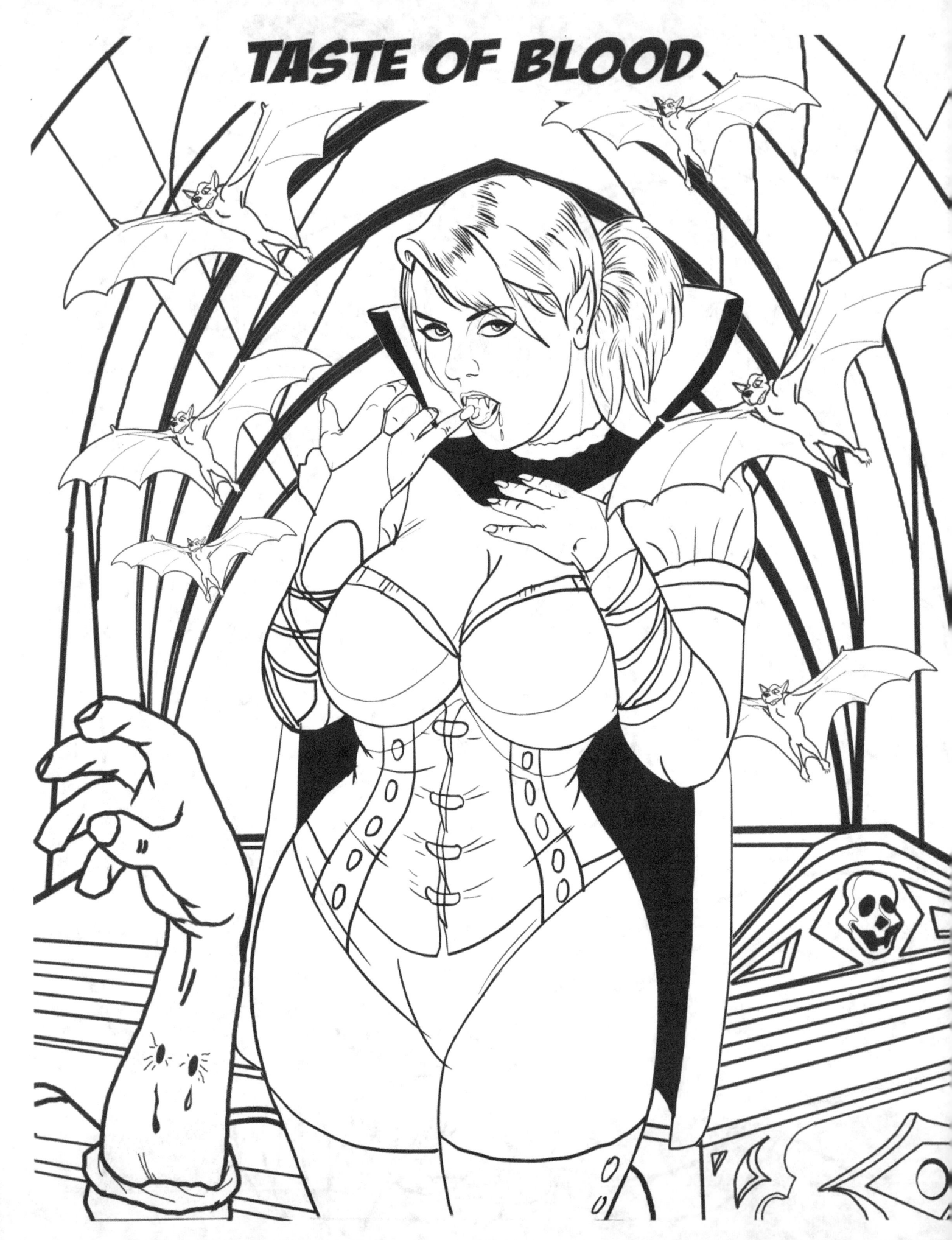

# VAMP OUT AT NIGHT

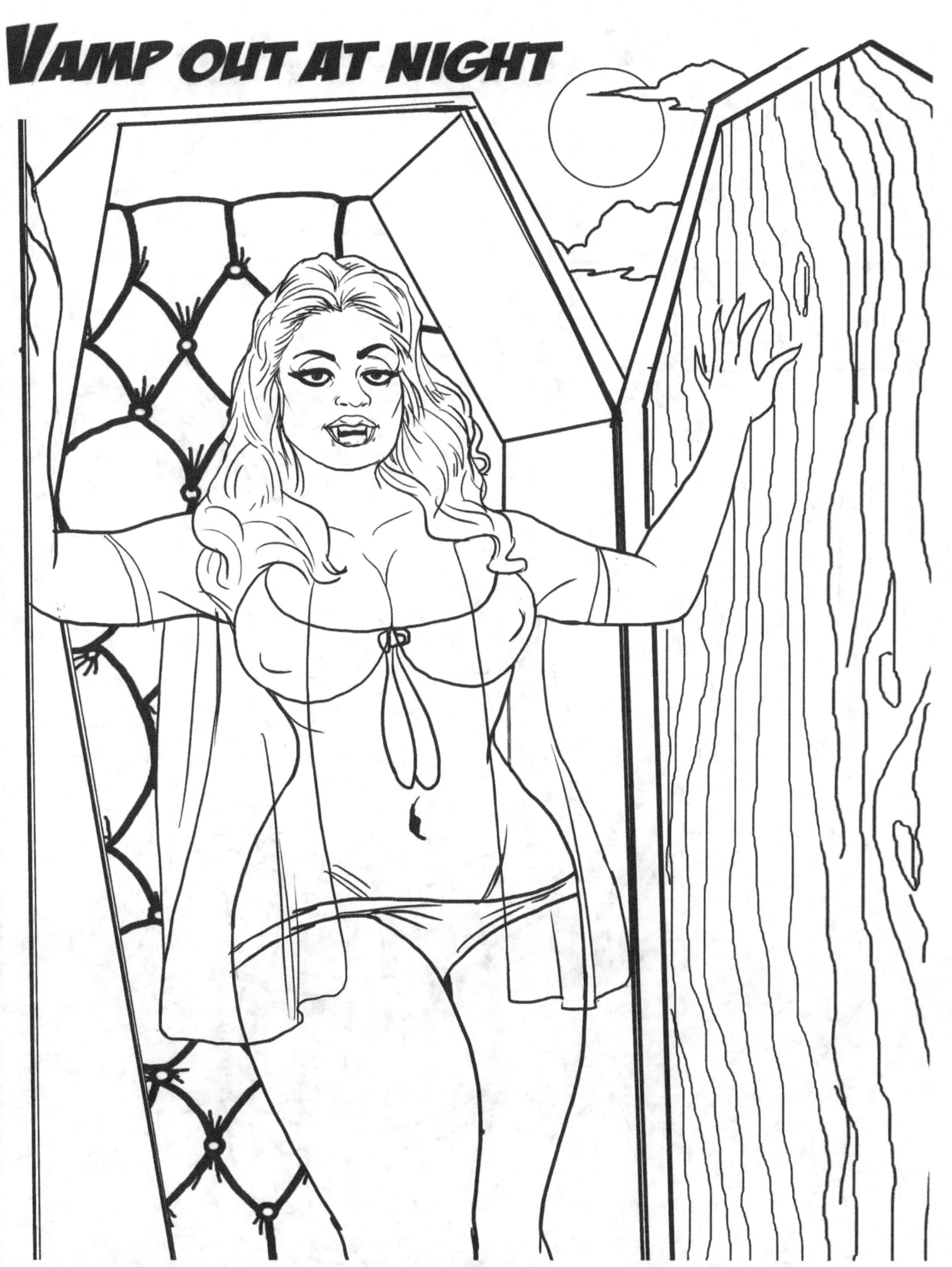

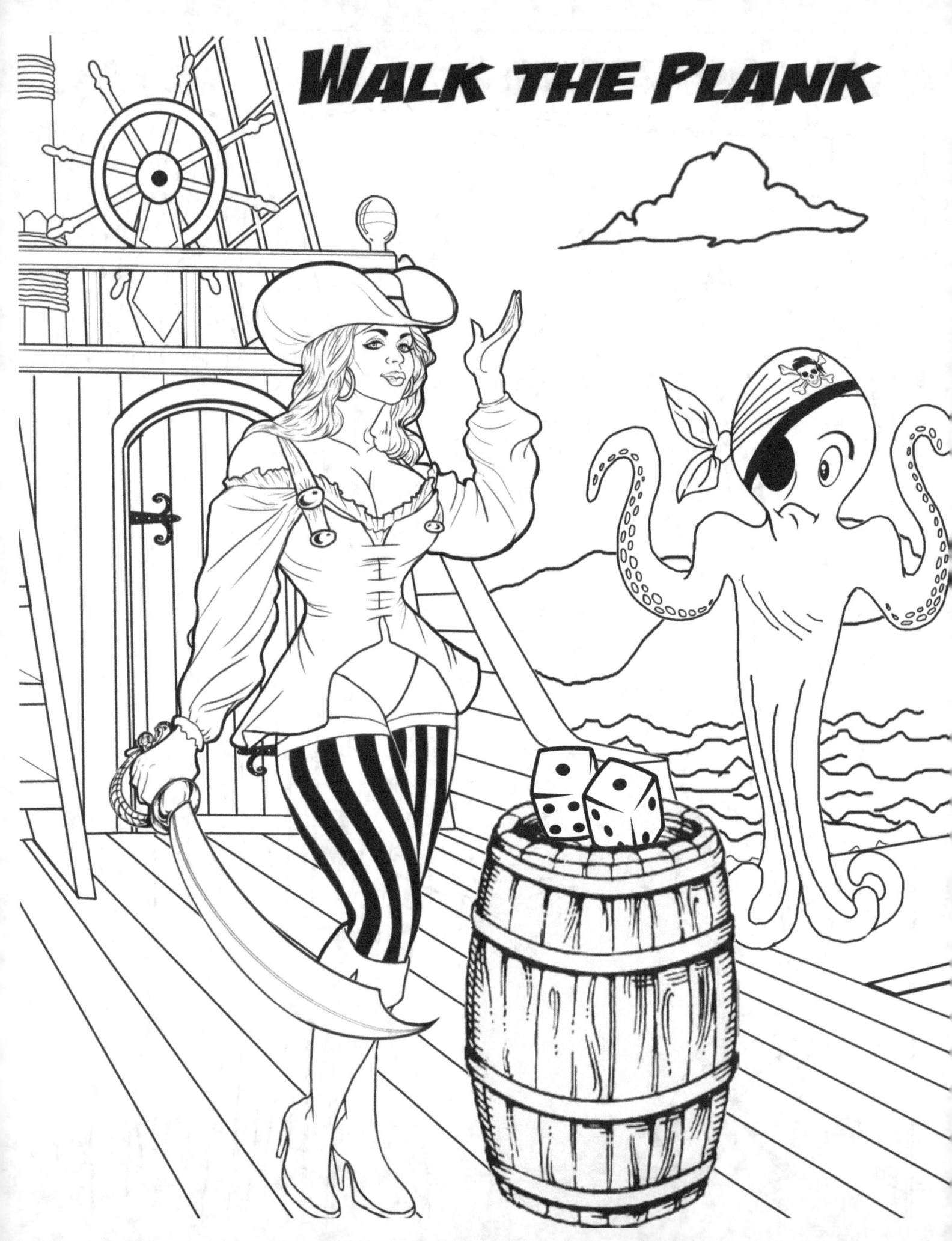

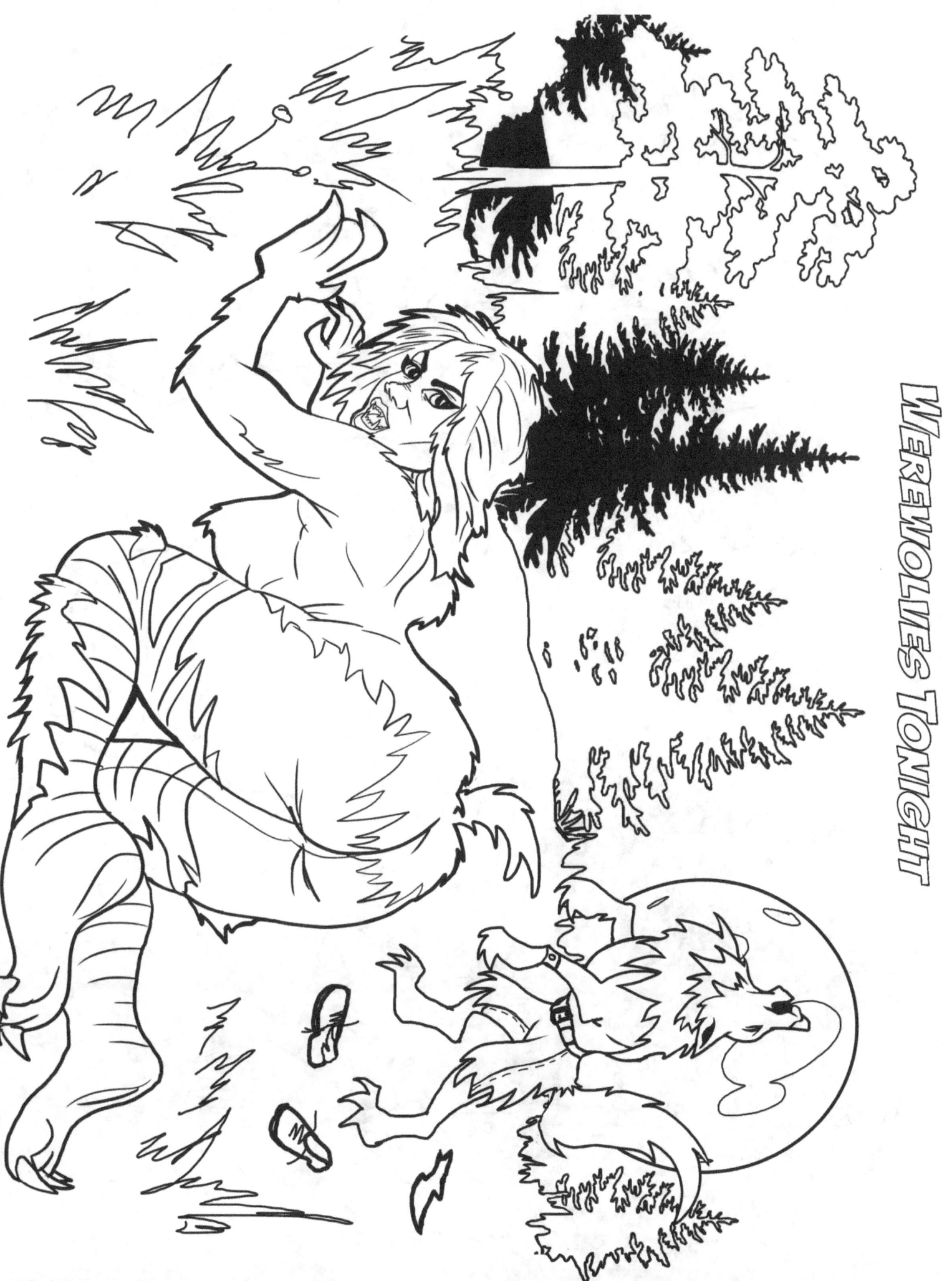

WEREWOLVES TONIGHT

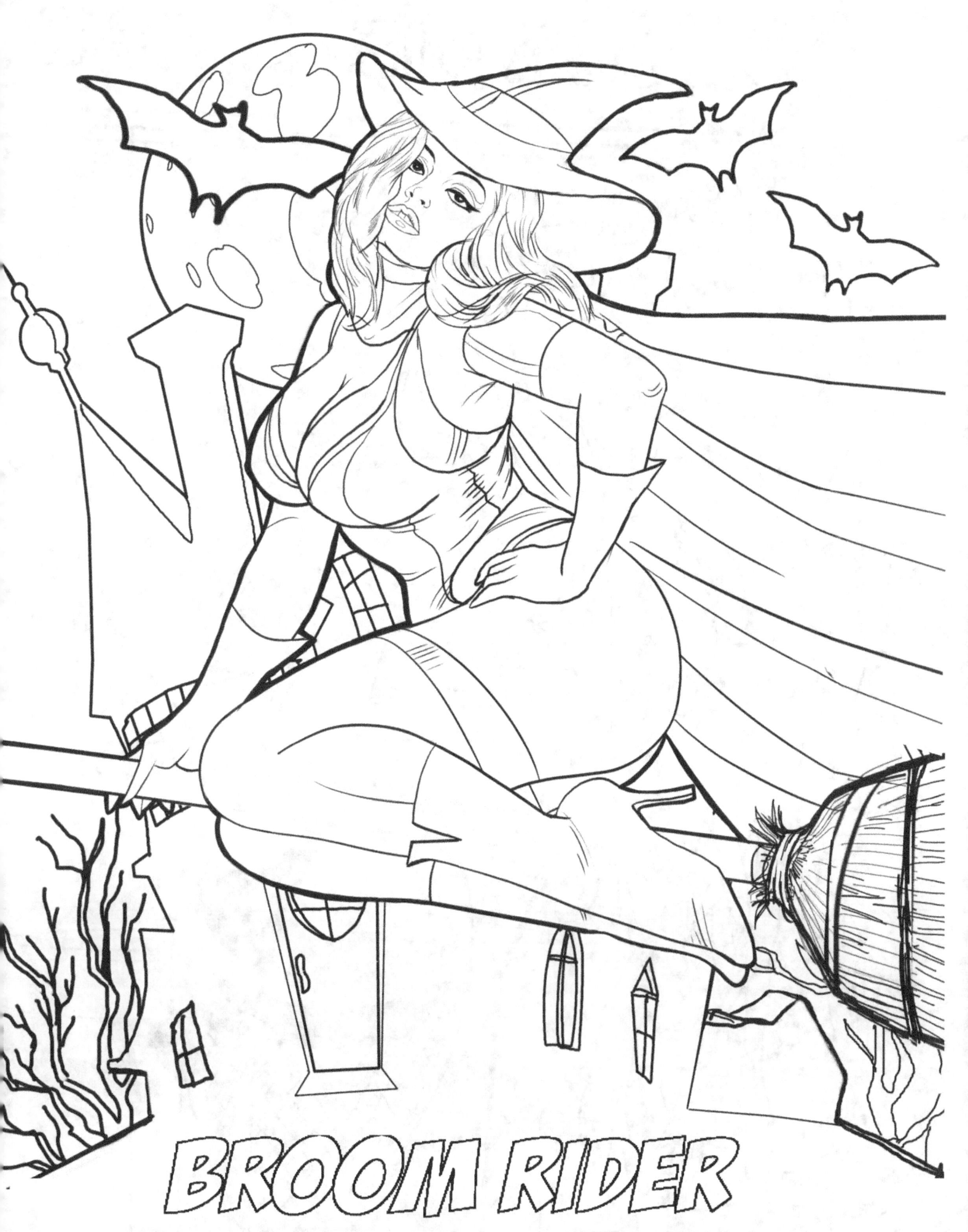

BROOM RIDER

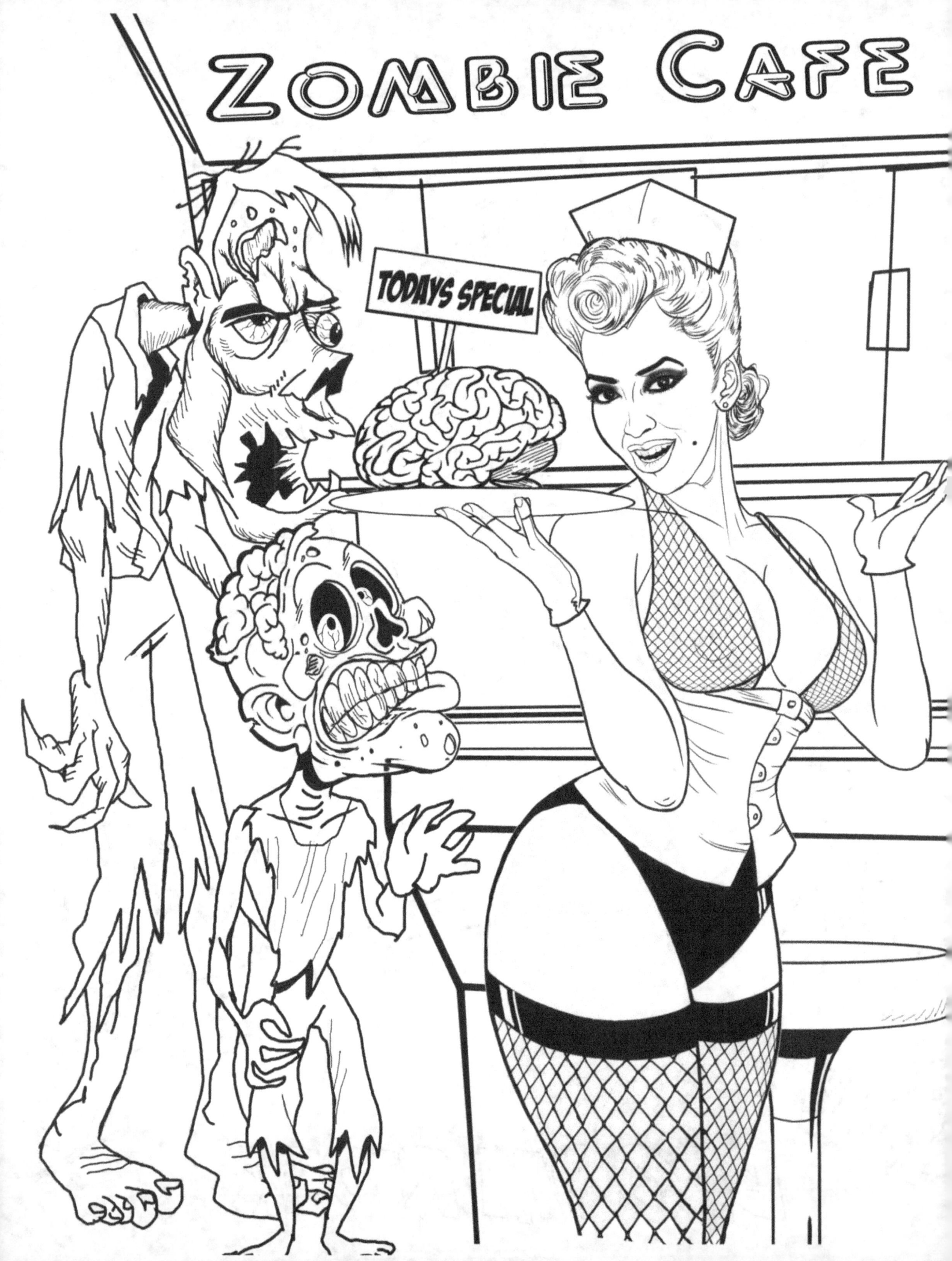

www.ingramcontent.com/pod-product-compliance
Lightning Source LLC
Chambersburg PA
CBHW081314180526
45170CB00007B/2706